Billpayers' Rights

"It is almost a case history of how every debt situation was solved without money and without pain to the debtor. It should be a best seller. Those in debt, and that is practically everyone, could buy a copy. And all manner of creditors and collection agencies will want the 'enemy intelligence.' "

— William Flynn, S. F. EXAMINER

"It contains all the information the average person needs to know about bankruptcy, wage attachments, car repossions, delinquent taxes, child support, credit cards and student loans."

— SAN FRANCISCO CONSUMER ACTION

"This book cuts through the bullshit, and, in a very readable fashion, gives you all you usually   need to know about the legal aspects of debts."

— BERKELEY BARB

"It's called a 'battle book,' but it's not a bugle call to bear arms or lead a revolt, but simply an informative source to help citizens deal with problems associated with a sagging ecomony."

— SAN JOSE MERCURY NEWS

Billpayers' Rights

BY ATTORNEYS
RALPH WARNER & STEPHEN ELIAS

Important: The information in this book changes rapidly and is subject to differing interpretations. It is up to you to check it thoroughly before relying on it. Neither the author nor publisher of this book makes any guarantees regarding the outcome of the uses to which this material is put.

NOLO PRESS • 950 Parker Street, Berkeley, CA 94710

Printing History

Nolo Press is committed to keeping its books up-to-date. Each new printing, whether or not it is called a new edition, has been completely revised to reflect the latest law changes. This book was printed and updated on the last date indicated below. Before you rely on information in it, you might wish to call Nolo Press, (415) 549-1976 to check whether a later printing or edition has been issued.

First Edition	April 1976
Second Edition	January 1975
Third Printing	July 1977
Third Edition	June 1979
Fourth Edition	July 1981
Fifth Edition	October 1983
Sixth Edition	January 1984
Seventh Edition	February 1986
Second Printing	July 1986

Printing History

Difference between new *editions* and *printings*:

New *printing* means there have been some minor changes, but usually not enough so that people will need to trade in or discard an earlier printing of the same edition. Obviously, this is a judgment call and any change, no matter how minor, might affect you.

New *edition* means one or more major--or a number of minor--law changes since the previous edition.

Stephanie Harolde	Production
Linda Allison	Illustrations
Keija Kimura	Book Design & Layout
Delta Lithograph	Printing

ISBN 0-87337-025-2

UPDATE SERVICE
■ Introductory Offer ■

Our books are as current as we can make them, but sometimes the laws do change between editions. You can read about law changes which may affect this book in the NOLO NEWS, a 16-page newspaper which we publish quarterly.

In addition to the Update Service, each issue contains comprehensive articles, about the growing self-help law movement as well as areas of the law that are sure to affect you. **(regular subscription rate is $7.00)**

To receive the next 4 issues of the NOLO NEWS, please send us $2.00.

Name _____

Address _____

_____

Send to: NOLO PRESS, 950 Parker St., Berkeley, CA 94710

Recycle Your Out-of-Date Books & Get One Third off your next purchase!

Using an old edition can be dangerous if information in it is wrong. Unfortunately, laws and legal procedure change often. To help you keep up to date we extend this offer. If you cut out and deliver to us the title portion of the cover of any old Nolo book we'll give you a 33% discount off the retail price of any new Nolo book. For example, if you have a copy of TENANTS' RIGHTS, 4th edition and want to trade it for the latest CALIFORNIA MARRIAGE AND DIVORCE LAW, send us the TENANTS' RIGHTS cover and a check for the current price of MARRIAGE & DIVORCE, less a 33% discount. Information on current prices and editions are listed in the Nolo News (see above box). Generally speaking, any book more than two years old is of questionable value. Books more than four or five years old are a menace.

OUT OF DATE = DANGEROUS

This offer is to individuals only.

Table of Contents

Thank You

For many years Peter Jan Honigsberg was the co-author of this book and many of Peter's graceful words still appear.

We are grateful for the generous help and many excellent suggestions of Ron Chase, the manager of the Co-op Credit Union in Berkeley. Thanks, too, to Papa Nolo, Ed Sherman, many of those words appear in Chapter 3; to Malcolm Roberts, everybody's favorite tax guru and to Katherine Galvin.

About The Authors . . .

Steve Elias received a law degree from Hastings College of Law in 1969. He practiced in California, New York and Vermont until 1983 when he decided to make a full-time career of helping non-lawyers understand the law. Steve is the author of Nolo's *Intellectual Property Law Dictionary* and co-author of *California Marriage and Divorce Law, Legal Research: How to Find and Understand the Law* and *WillWriter,* a computer package for making simple wills (all published by Nolo Press. In addition Steve has edited a number of other Nolo books, including *Media Law* (Katherine Galvin), *How to Copyright Software* (M.J. Salone) and *Patent It Yourself* (David Pressman).

At present Steve teaches legal research for a local paralegal institute and the Nolo Press Seminar series, and is working on the family law portion of his law dictionary and *Make Your Own Contract,* a book containing simple tear-out contracts.

RALPH "JAKE" WARNER lives in Berkeley, California. He is concerned with consumer law reform with the goal that everyone will have equal access to our legal system. A people's law pioneer, he helped found Nolo Press and has been active in creating several other alternatives to our constipated and over-priced legal system. Jake is the co-author of *The California Tenants' Handbook, The Living Together Kit, Everybody's Guide to Small Claims Court,* and editor of *The People's Law Review,* a Whole Earth Catalog of the self-help law movement.

$ $ $ $ $

Introduction

Here is a book about the problems that come with owing money and being unable or unwilling to pay it. We tell you exactly what and who you are up against and how you can best deal with your situation. The information given here is known by every credit bureau, bill collector, loan shark, and collection attorney in the country. They use this information consciously and often cynically to squeeze every possible cent out of you. Here, we give you the knowledge to avoid the squeeze where possible, and in many cases to exert a little pressure of your own.

At a time when consumption has become a god and we are taught from birth that large quantities of shiny gadgets will make us happy, most people are in debt.

Indeed much of our society seems to be built around the buying and selling of more and more expensive nonsense and might well have a nervous breakdown if people showed signs of not buying things on credit. For most of us it doesn't take much in the way of illness, accident, loss of work, or domestic trouble, etc., to tip the scales so that our burden of debt becomes impossible to carry. When this happens and the notices, phone calls, threats, wage attachments, repossessions, and all the rest begin, we quickly learn how society treats those who fall even a little behind in their ability to pay for their possessions. It isn't very nice. Simply stated, it's brutal, ruthless, and usually effective.

California law has always been favorable to creditors. In the past several years, however, the legislature and courts--at the urgings of consumer and legal aid organizations--have provided greater protection for the person in debt. Here we give you all of that information so that you can use it to protect yourself and plan sensibly for the future.

In writing this book we have had some trouble figuring out the best way to organize all the material. This is partly because different types of debts are treated differently under the law. But it is also partly because people approach life from so many different directions. One person is mostly worried about whether she can wipe out a student loan in bankruptcy, while someone else only cares about the repossession of a pickup truck. All necessary information has been included, but perhaps not in the order you might have chosen. Please pay close attention to the Table of Contents. You will find it to be a good outline of the whole subject, as well as a direction finder for any individual problem. There is nothing hard about the rules and regulations that we discuss, but some overlap a bit and others are a little sticky and technical. You need to relax and get the complete picture before you make any decisions. So read the whole book through and then reread the parts that are of special interest to you.

Some people will feel that this book is overly biased in favor of debtors and that the existence of unscrupulous debtors and honest creditors is overlooked. To this charge we plead guilty. In these pages the creditor appears rather regularly as an ogre. We do not mean that "badness" is necessarily in the nature of creditors. But, since we are writing about problems as seen from the debtor's point of view, we do focus upon all the foul deeds that creditors have been known to do, including misleading advertising, exorbitant interest rates, shoddy goods, and brutal collection practices. Yes, this book is purposely oriented around debtors' problems. Creditors have associations, lobbyists, lawyers and legislators to protect their interests, while debtors have almost no resources. This book is designed to change this imbalance. In short--this is a battle book.

chapter 1

$ $ $ $ $ $

General Things to Know

A. It's Not as Bad as You Think

Many people believe that once they get into debt all sorts of terrible things will happen to them. In fact very few of these imagined horrors exist. Being in debt may be unpleasant, but it is not a catastrophe. To start with, you can't be sent to jail for not paying your debts whether you have the money to do so or not.* Debtors' prison no longer exists. In addition, most of your property, including the equity in your dwelling up to $30,000 if you are single and not yet 65, $45,000 if you are a family, and $55,000 if you are over 65 or physically or mentally disabled and unable to work, your clothing, your furniture and one or more motor vehicles with a combined equity of $1,200 are exempt under California law and can't be taken from you to pay other debts.** (There are a lot more exemptions in addition to the few mentioned here; see Chapters 10, 11 and 12 for a complete discussion.)

Many types of income are also exempt from attachment, including unemployment, disability, workers' compensation, social security and welfare benefits. Wages can be attached, but only up to 25% of your paycheck and, if you can show that you and/or your family need

---

* You can be sent to jail under criminal laws for not paying spousal support (alimony) or child support if, and only if, you have the ability to support and refuse to do so. See Chapter 17.

** Of course, no exemption law protects you from losing an item where you have failed to make payments on the item itself, and the item has been put up for security. See Chapter 5.

your pay to live decently, you may be able to get even this portion returned to you (see Chapter 10).*

There is no need to put up with harassment by bill collectors. There are now strict rules as to what collectors can and can't do. We will teach you all you need to know about enforcing these rules in Chapter 7.

You may decide after reading what follows that your burden of debt is too heavy to ever pay off. If so, you can file bankruptcy and wipe out your bills entirely, or you can arrange to pay them over a long period of time under a federal Chapter 13 plan (see Chapter 18).

B. Anxiety

Most of us are raised to believe that a person should pay his debts and that it is somehow immoral not to. We are told that successful people have lots of money and possessions, and that people who have neither are failures. This view of life is reinforced often by a society which commonly hands out places in the pecking order solely on the basis of how much money a person has. Okay, so what else is new?--you know all that. But know too that bill collectors are carefully trained to exploit your guilt feelings and are consciously trying to make you feel as miserable as possible. They figure that if they make you feel anxious enough, you will scramble to get the money you owe them somehow. If you have a heart attack or develop an ulcer in the meantime--well, that's your problem.

When bills pile up and there is no

money to pay them, most people get anxious. Their minds return time and time again to the problem of their debts and the fact that they can't be paid. Of course, this is a waste of time, but then worrying usually is. Even people who understand intellectually that being a good human being and a rich one are not the same thing, that wealth is as likely to interfere with humanity as to enhance it, get trapped by anxiety. They do this even though they realize that they are hurting themselves far more than the bill collector can.

Getting on top of anxiety and stopping the fretting away of one's life over money worries is a hard, but necessary, job. We will help you with some of it by explaining simply what you are and are not up against, and giving you some ideas as to what you can do to help yourself. We can't do the whole job for you, however. Only you can understand that being a loving, wise, giving human being has nothing to do with how much money you owe. Only you can clear yourself of the programming of a million Madison Avenue advertisements and realize that owing a few bills is not the end of the world. Cheer up--wallowing in guilt is a waste of life's beautiful energy.

C. What About Your Credit?

The chances are great that you have encountered the need for a good credit

---

* Wages can be attached in excess of this amount to satisfy child and spousal support debts (Chapter 17). There are also special rules for taxes. See Chapter 16.

rating at some point in your life. At one time, good credit was necessary to obtain loans, goods on time, and to purchase a home, but generally was unnecessary for most other normal life needs. This has changed dramatically.

The ability of computers to store massive amounts of information about people and provide instant access to anyone willing to pay for it has made a good credit rating important in a great variety of new circumstances. Indeed, in many situations, having a good credit rating is the only way to prove good character. A few examples will demonstrate this point.

In most urban areas, rental housing is largely managed by property management firms. When you attempt to rent an apartment, you are usually required to fill out an application which asks for credit references. In all too many cases, the absence of such references will put you at a great competitive disadvantage in respect to other applicants. A bad credit rating will probably be fatal to your efforts. When you think of it, your credit status should have little to do with your getting the apartment, since you are generally required to pay rent in advance. In fact, however, your very character is being judged by reference to your credit.

In addition to apartment rentals, a bad credit rating may prevent you from 1) purchasing a house, 2) cashing a check, 3) ordering goods or services by phone, 4) renting a car, 5) obtaining emergency care at many hospitals unless you are insured, and 6) starting your own business (because of the need for short term credit in most business situations). There are many other examples as well, and they are growing every day.

Throughout this book, we attempt to specify the effects which any particular debt handling remedy may have on your credit. In some situations, you will have to decide for yourself whether you

would rather use a lawful remedy and potentially damage your credit rating (bankruptcy is an example) or retain a good (or at least neutral) credit rating at the cost of foregoing your rights. Often your only practical choice will be to follow one or another legal procedure to protect yourself from aggressive creditors, as you simply will not have the financial resources to repay your debts.

NOTE: Having a good credit rating does not mean that you should use it to fuel the rampant American consumerism. While a good credit rating will certainly open many doors, actually using credit to buy your favorite toys may put you in worse financial shape than if you had bad credit to start with. Our suggestion: strive for a good credit rating, but don't use it except as a character reference. End of sermon.

D. Legal Jargon Definitions

As you read further, you will come upon a few terms that you may not be familiar with, or which may have technical legal meanings different from the common ones. Our aim is to simplify, to speak plainly to those without legal training, but it is necessary to use some legal jargon. We will define most unfamiliar terms as we go along, but there are a few terms we should deal with right now.

ACCELERATION CLAUSE: Allows the remaining balance due on a contract to be immediately due. Usually this occurs when you miss a payment.

AMORTIZATION: Repaying a loan or other debt in installments.

BALLOON PAYMENT: The final payment of an installment contract which is larger than the others. Beware of this one.

COLLATERAL: Additional security given to get a loan. For example, if you buy a dishwasher, a finance company may have you list all your furniture on the finance agreement as extra security. If you don't make the payments, the finance company will threaten to take (repossess) all your furniture as well as the dishwasher.

CO-SIGNER: The best one-word definition that we know for most co-signers is "IDIOT." A co-signer is a person who by signing his name fully obligates himself to pay another person's debt if that person fails to do so, whatever the reason.* The co-signer gets none of the benefits from the transaction (usually some sort of loan) and often, all of the burdens. Should the primary debtor default, the co-signer can be sued if he doesn't pay the debt voluntarily, and is subject to having his wages attached if he doesn't pay the judgment. A person should co-sign only if he is fully prepared to pay the debt if the debtor defaults.

CREDITOR: As used by us, this means a person to whom money is owed. A creditor may be the person who actually lent the money, or he may be someone like the bill collector who is collecting the money for the original creditor.

DEBTOR: A person who owes money.

DOWN PAYMENT (deposits): Money you put down to bind a deal. Down payments are generally not refundable if you back out unless you have a good reason, but generally are refundable if the other party fails to perform.

EQUITY: The dollar amount of your

home or other property that you own. On a home, figure your equity by taking the sale value of your home and then subtracting the amount you still owe on your mortgage and the amount it would cost to make the sale. For example, if your home could be sold for $40,000, you owe $10,000 on your mortgage, and it would cost $2,000 to sell (realtor's commissions, etc.), then your equity is $28,000.

JUDGMENT PROOF: This means that you simply don't have to worry about debts because you have nothing that anyone can legally take away from you. If after reading this book you conclude that you are judgment proof, you can relax. A family would be judgment proof if, for example, they live on social security, have less than $500 on deposit in an account in which payments by the Social Security Administration are directly deposited, have one or more motor vehicles with an aggregate equity of $1,200 or less, have normal amounts of clothing and furniture, and a dwelling which you occupy with an equity of $45,000 or less. You will learn a great deal about being judgment proof as we go along. At this point, we just want you to be familiar with the term. IMPORTANT: It is possible to be judgment proof now, but have to pay judgments, including attorney fees and court costs, later on. This would be the case in the example given above if the family was given or had inherited money or property or the head of the family went back to work.

PERSONAL PROPERTY: All property other than land and buildings attached to land. Cars, bank accounts, wages, furniture, mobile homes, insurance policies, etc., are all personal property.

PROMISSORY NOTE: A written promise to pay.

REAL PROPERTY: Land and the buildings built on the land. Your home is real property.

---

* If the principal parties to a contract change the terms of the agreement without the approval of the co-signer, he or she is no longer responsible. Also, any defenses that a principal to a contract may raise may be raised by the co-signer. See Cal. Civil Code Section 2819; WEXLER V. MCLUCAS 48 CA3 Supp. 9 (1975).

chapter 2

$ $ $ $ $ $

Debts You Feel You Don't Owe

This book deals primarily with being over your head with debts you feel you legally owe. We do not spend much time on situations where you feel you have been screwed over by dishonest salesmen or creditors. This is the subject for a book on consumer rights. But we will review briefly this area here and outline several helpful approaches.

Often disputes arise between the buyer and the seller of goods and services over such things as unexplained credit charges, excessive interest, shoddy work or merchandise, failure to perform work or supply goods in the time promised, and the delivery of goods or services different from those promised. Sometimes these disputes involve simple misunderstandings between honest people and sometimes they involve misrepresentations or outright fraud. Your first

job is to get your head clear as to exactly what sort of situation you face. Ask yourself the following questions:

a) Am I dealing with a reputable person or corporation?

b) Have I done anything to contribute to the misunderstanding?

c) Is there a reasonable chance that some sort of compromise can be worked out?

Don't let your own anger, no matter how justifiable, blind you to the situation you face and the best way to deal with it.

WARRANTIES! You are entitled to rely on any written warranty that comes with a product. You should also know that under state law (Civil Code Section 1791.1) many products (mostly machines, appliances, and motor vehicles) are covered by an implied warranty of "merchantability" and "fitness."* This means that the product is reasonably workable (isn't defective) and, if the seller knows what the buyer plans to use it for, will reasonably fill this need. The period of time for which an implied warranty is good is the same as any written warranty that comes with a product if there is one (but in no case is shorter than 60 days). If there is no written warranty stating a shorter period than one year, the implied warranty period is one year. If an express or implied warranty is breached, the consumer may be entitled to a refund or damages. For details, see the California Civil Code Sections 1791 to 1797.5. Products clearly marked "as is" or "with all defects" are not covered by warranty.

NOTE: California law grants people a three-day cooling off period on door-to-door sales if the amount involved is $25 or more. Notify the creditor (use certified mail) in writing before midnight of the third business day after signing the contract that you wish to cancel and they must return your money within 10 days, Civil Code Section 1689.5 et seq.

A. If You Have Been Defrauded

If you believe you have been cheated, you should immediately let several county, state, and federal agencies know about it. They may be able to help you directly and at least will have the information necessary for moving against

---

* Special warranty rules affecting defects in mobile homes, recreational vehicles, and manufactured housing are found in Civil Code Sections 1797.1-1997.6. They allow a year after purchase to assert claims of substantial defects against either the manufacturer or dealer. The defects must be fixed at the site of the home.

the crooks. Law enforcement in the consumer fraud area is not as good as it should be, but it's vastly better than it was a few years ago. Once you decide that fraud may be involved, the faster you move the better. Do not pay anything in a situation where you believe you have been swindled. Instead, you should immediately notify:

1. The District Attorney in the county in which you live. Call them and ask for a person who handles consumer fraud complaints. They will send you a complaint form.

2. State of California, Office of the Attorney General, Public Inquiry Unit, 1515 "K" St., Sacramento, California 95814 or call the Public Inquiry Unit on their toll-free number [800] 952-5225. (Your complaint will be routed through this office to the deputy attorney general most familiar with your area of concern. You can get a complaint form by calling the Attorney General in Los Angeles, San Francisco, or Sacramento.)

3. The Federal Trade Commission, Room 13209 Federal Building, 11000 Wilshire Boulevard, Los Angeles, California 90024 OR 450 Golden Gate Avenue, Box 36005, San Francisco, California 94102. (It's best to call first and get a complaint form.)

4. There are dozens of state and federal offices that are geared to handling individual areas of concern. For example, there is one office that you complain to about optometrists and another about osteopaths. See your metropolitan phone book white pages under Consumer Complaint and Protection Coordinators and you will find many listings, or call [916] 445-1254.

IMPORTANT: Keep all contracts, letters, guarantees, etc., that relate to the dispute and try to get all promises in writing. Business people keep records or they don't stay in business long. To protect yourself, so must you.

Be sure to keep copies of letters you send to the creditors.

B. Misunderstandings Between Buyer and Seller

All too often services are not performed properly or goods turn out to be defective or are not delivered on time. We are all familiar with the car that falls apart a few days after purchase,* the roof that leaks more after repair than before, and the merchandise that shows up six months after you don't want it any more.

1. When You Have Paid

If you have paid for goods or services before you learn they are somehow not right, you should first ask the dealer to fix the problem. Be sure to consult any guarantee or written contract to see if these help you. If you have lost these documents, request copies from the seller of the goods. If after complaining to those concerned about the problem, no fair compromise is agreed to, you will need to assert yourself. Remember, some creditors will promise you the moon and deliver nothing. Don't let anyone jive you too long. Your first step is to write a letter setting out your contentions in detail. Send a copy of the letter to any state, federal or local agency interested in the area and let the creditor know you have done so. This puts the seller on notice that you are serious. It is also a good idea to contact the original manufacturer of a product

---

* Civil Code Section 1793.2 [the "Lemon Law"] provides that if within one year, or 12,000 miles of the purchase of a new car, the same nonconformity has been subject to repair four or more times by the manufacturer or its agents for a cumulative total of more than 30 calendar days, the manufacturer must either replace the goods, or reimburse the buyer.

if your dispute is with a middleman. General Electric, for example, has a real interest in seeing that a hardware store which sells their toasters treats people honestly.

---

315 Main Street
Oakland, California
March 18, 19__

Over the Rainbow Used Chariots
331 10th Street
Berkeley, California 94710

On March 10, 19__ I purchased a 1980 Chevrolet from your company, and paid you $3,000 cash. You specifically told me that the car had only been driven 20,000 miles, that it had been completely checked by your mechanics and that, to the best of your knowledge, the car was in good shape.

On March 14, 19__ I drove the car to Stockton, California. While there, the entire tail pipe and muffler fell off and the car started smoking. On investigation, I found that the tail pipe clamps were missing and that the tail pipe itself was secured to the bottom of the car with a piece of twisted wire. I also discovered that the engine contained a heavy grade of truck oil, apparently so that the existence of two badly burned valves would not be noticed.

Because the car was unsafe to drive back to Berkeley, I took it to the Chevrolet dealership in Stockton. They made the necessary repairs and charged me $802.00. I enclose a photocopy of the bill. When I returned to Berkeley, I called your office and asked you to pay this amount. In that conversation, you treated me rudely and said you would not pay me a penny.

Please send me the $802.00 immediately. If I don't hear from you by March 23, I plan to take legal action.

Very truly yours,

Helen West

copies sent to:

1. District Investigator, Department of Motor Vehicles
(address of nearest Motor Vehicles Office)

2. Consumer Fraud Section, District Attorney of _____ County
3. State of California, Department of Consumer Affairs

If conversation and a letter or two fail, you have to get serious, or drop the matter. Only you can decide whether the dispute is worth the continuing hassle. Assuming you decide to persevere, it may be wise to see a lawyer at this stage if your claim is for a lot of money. He or she may be able to write a letter or make a phone call that will solve the problem. Unfortunately, there is often a big psychological difference between getting a letter from you and getting one on legal letterhead (see Chapter 3). If a large amount of money is involved, you may want to retain a lawyer to start a lawsuit in Municipal Court (up to $25,000) or Superior Court (over $25,000). But be sure you understand clearly how much this will cost before you get involved in it. Consider too, that lawsuits can be lost and that it is sometimes easier to win the suit than it is to collect on the judgment.

You may also want to consider suing in Small Claims Court. No lawyers are allowed in this court and you can sue for any amount up to $1,500.* If your claim is greater than this amount, you will either have to waive the excess or not use Small Claims Court. The rules for Small Claims Court are contained in California Code of Civil Procedure Sections 116-117.20. This book is available at most public libraries and at all county law libraries. Also, you will want to see EVERYBODY'S GUIDE TO SMALL CLAIMS COURT, Warner, Nolo Press (see back of this book).

To sue in Small Claims court, go to your local municipal courthouse and find the Clerk of the Small Claims Court. The clerk is required by law to fill out a complaint form for you if you so re-

---

* We favor legislation to greatly increase this amount. People should be able to handle their own disputes without lawyers at least up to $5,000 (in many situations $10,000 would be reasonable).

quest. On the form you state how much money you are owed and the reason for the claim. After you file the form with the clerk, the clerk will advise you as to how to best serve the defendant with an order for him to appear in court on a certain date and time. Often, but not always, service can be accomplished by mail. Your court date will be not more than 40 days nor less than 10 days if the defendant lives within your county, or not more than 70 days nor less than 30 days if he lives in another county.

Trials in Small Claims Court are informal. Simply bring all records, including photographs, letters, contracts, etc., that you believe back up your case. Also, bring all witnesses who have first-hand information about the facts in dispute. Don't be afraid of the court. Go down a few days before and watch a few cases if you are at all nervous. It's a very simple procedure and you will see that people do best when they tell their story briefly and logically and present witnesses and documents in an orderly way. If you tell the judge a long story, she will get bored and possibly irritated. Remember, she hears many cases every day and will not be particularly excited about yours. The more long-winded you are, the more likely she is to start thinking about her lunch.

2. When You Have Not Paid

Sometime in elementary school you probably heard the expression "possession is nine-tenths of the law." After more years of law school than we care to think about, we can tell you that this grade school wisdom is very often right on. If you are unhappy about goods or services you ordered and have a legitimate reason for your concern, don't pay. You are in possession of the money and no one can get it from you short of a law suit. Law suits are unpleasant and expensive to start. It is in the seller's interest to make any reasonable compromise with you in order to get paid and get the matter settled without court action.

Should you receive a bill which you believe to be unfair either in whole or in part, it is wise to call or write the company involved.

---

180 Phoenix Avenue
Belmont, California
May 10, 19___

Honest John Paints
1515 Olive Street
Sacramento, California

Dear Honest John:

Today I received a bill for $750 for painting. I have no intention of paying it, as the work was not done.

On April 14, 19___ you sent an untrained painter to my house. In the first hour he spilled paint on my rug, started to apply enamel paint meant for woodwork to the ceiling, and kicked my dog. I requested that he leave, and he did so.

If you persist in bothering me about this bill, I plan to file a formal complaint with the consumer fraud section of the District Attorney's Office and will consult an attorney concerning legal rights as far as suing you for damages.

Very truly yours,

5377 Sweet William St.
Mendocino, California
May 10, 19___

Honest John Paints
1515 Olive St.
Sacramento, California

Dear Honest John:

I received your bill today for $750 for painting my living room. I do not feel that I owe you this amount.

It is true that we signed a contract saying that you would get $750 for the work, but it was clearly understood that you were to do the work in a careful, businesslike way. Instead, you sent out an inexperienced painter who did the following:

1. Dripped paint on a rug valued at $400, ruining it;

2. Left paint streaks on windows which took me five hours to clean off with a razor blade.

I am willing to pay you $350 for the work done, and will send you a check for that amount as soon as you send me a corrected bill.

Very truly yours,

IMPORTANT: If you believe that you owe part, but not all, of a bill, it is often psychologically wise to send a check or money order for the amount you feel you owe, along with your letter explaining your position. If you do this, write on the back of the check, where the endorsement would normally go, a statement that cashing the check constitutes full settlement of all debts between you and the other party. In the first letter above, the back of your check would look like this:

Cashing of this check by
Honest John Paints
constitutes full satisfaction
of all debts owed to them

If you can't work out any sort of compromise and you keep being hassled by a creditor, it is important that you pay attention to what is happening and protect yourself. You will want to do one or more of the following:

a) Complain to at least one of the agencies listed in Section A of this chapter or in the Consumer Complaint and Protection Coordinators' section of your metropolitan phone book white pages.

b) If a lot of money is involved, consider consulting an attorney for advice and perhaps for help in compromising the claim (see Chapter 3).

c) Fight any lawsuit that is filed against you.

C. If a Third Party Owns Your Debt

It often happens that the original person with whom you deal (say a furniture dealer) sells your debt obligation to a third party (say a bank). You now owe monthly payments to the bank. But what happens if something major goes wrong with the furniture? Can you raise the claim against the bank and perhaps refuse to pay them until some fair adjustment is made? The answer is generally, "Yes," you can normally assert claims against third parties. As we stated earlier, a good general rule is not to pay for goods or services that are defective until some adjustment is made. Be sure to notify everyone involved in the dispute (manufacturer, seller, finance company or bank, etc.) of why you are refusing to pay. Keep carbon or xerox copies of all communications.

D. If You Are Sued

Please turn to Chapter 8 which contains a full discussion of law suits and how to protect yourself.

chapter 3

$ $ $ $ $ $

Lawyers and Credit Counselors

A. Lawyers—Doing Your Own Research

Within the past decade people have become more sophisticated in dealing with legal problems. Many people now take their own case to court--not only to Small Claims Court but also Municipal and Superior Court. See Chapter 8. But whether you intend to handle your own case or not, you should know all the laws which apply to it. This book is your beginning. But sometimes your situation will not be fully covered. So where do you go next?

Rather than run right to a lawyer, you may want to research the problem yourself. Researching the law is actually easier than you might think. The law books are, for the most part, logically indexed, and complement each other. It shouldn't take you long to figure out how to search through the

Civil Code (or any other statute) or look up and read a case. Law, though cloaked in mystery, is actually pretty easy to unveil.

Law materials are available in law school libraries and county law libraries which are located in the principal county courthouses.* The county law libraries are open to the public; law school libraries may have some restrictions; you'll have to check. City public libraries and college libraries also have some law materials, but are not as complete.

There are two useful texts written expressly for consumers (as well as law students) on how to use law materials, LEGAL RESEARCH: HOW TO FIND AND UNDER-

---

* The majority of California laws affecting the debtor are found in either the Civil Code (C.C.) or the Code of Civil Procedure (C.C.P.). Both are available at libraries or may be purchased from Nolo Press (see back of this book).

STAND THE LAW, by Stephen Elias, published by Nolo Press (order information in back of book), and GILBERTS: LEGAL RESEARCH AND WRITING, by Peter Jan Honigsberg (available at any law bookstore).

1. What Lawyers Can Do for You

There are four basic ways a lawyer can help you:

a. CONSULTATION AND ADVICE: The lawyer can listen to the details of your situation, analyze it for you, and advise you on your position and best plan of action. Ideally, she will give you more than just conclusions--she can educate you about your whole situation and tell you all the alternatives available from which you can make your own choices. This kind of service is the least expensive since it only involves an official call and a little time. A charge of more than $50 for a consultation might be considered excessive. Find out the fee before you go in.

b. NEGOTIATION: The lawyer can use her special talents, knowledge and experience to help you negotiate with the creditor to your best advantage. In case of serious problems, she can do this more successfully than you, especially if you are at odds with the creditor, or if your creditor has an attorney. Without spending much of her own time, she can often accomplish a lot through a letter or phone call. Receiving a message on an attorney's letterhead is, in itself, often very sobering to a creditor. She knows you mean business. A lawyer can sometimes possess considerable skill as a negotiator. Also, if bad turns to worse, a lawyer can often bluff by threatening legal action. You can then decide at a later time whether to actually pursue it. In

trying to compromise debts (see Chapter 7), a lawyer can be particularly helpful, since the creditor knows that she is the person who would file a bankruptcy.

c. PRIVATE ATTORNEYS: If you don't know an attorney who can be trusted and can't get a reliable recommendation from a friend, you have a problem. While you might be lucky and randomly pick an attorney who matches your needs perfectly, you might just as easily wind up paying too much for too little. Here are some suggestions that should make your search a little easier:

●We do not recommend referral panels set up by local bar associations. Lawyers are supposed to be screened on their expertise in consumer matters, but often the screening is minimal. There is usually a small fee for an initial consultation. You may get a good referral from these panels, but be sure to question the lawyer whose name you are given about his or her qualifications and sympathy to your rights as a consumer;

●Check with local consumer organizations to see if they can recommend someone. In Northern California, Consumer Group Legal Services of Berkeley offers good quality legal help at a fair price;

●Shop around by calling different law offices and stating your problem. Ask them how much it would cost for a visit. Try to talk to a lawyer personally to get an idea of how friendly and sympathetic he or she is to your concerns;

Remember, lawyers whose offices and life styles are reasonably simple are more likely to help you for less money than lawyers who feel naked unless wearing a $500 outfit. You should be able to find an attorney willing to discuss your problems for $50 - $75.

B. Debt Consolidation Services

Much of what passes for credit counseling is no more than a front for loan sharking. The idea is to lend you more money at outrageous rates (up to 30% per year), rather than help you get out of debt. Debt consolidation loans definitely fall into this category. These loans are normally made by finance or thrift companies, whose consolidation loan practices should, in our opinion, be outlawed by state law. Consolidation outfits put all your debts together and charge only one payment--one impossible payment. If you are already in the hole, don't try to get out by digging deeper.

C. Credit Counseling

There is one counseling service in the state that we can recommend. It is Consumer Credit Counselors. We include a list of their offices below. C.C.C. is a nonprofit organization set up and sponsored by large respectable creditors such as department stores, banks, etc. They want you to pay your debts and feel that they will benefit in the long run by giving you counseling as to how to do it. They hate the notion of bankruptcy, as all creditors do. If you are interested in bankruptcy, read Chapter 18 and stay away from C.C.C. However, if you feel you can pay your debts with a little time and are willing to work out a detailed budget and stick to it, C.C.C. can help you. They have a plan allowing you to make one or two payments per month to them. They then divide the money among your creditors, after getting the creditors to agree to extend your time to pay. Because C.C.C. is set up by the creditors, it has a lot of influence. It can stop wage attachments and often get interest and late charges wiped out altogether. The only charge for this service is 6.5% of the money paid creditors each month--or $20-- whichever is less. There is no charge at all for counseling, making a budget, etc.

You can get free information about the services offered by contacting any of the following offices:

C.C.C. of San Francisco
and the Peninsula
1275 Market St. (Lobby Floor)
San Francisco, CA 94103
(415) 431-0510

C.C.C. of Santa Clara Valley
1825 De La Cruz Blvd., Ste. 8
Santa Clara, CA 95050
(408) 988-7881

C.C.C. of Sacramento
1815 J Street
Sacramento, CA 95814
(916) 444-0740

C.C.C. of San Diego
P.O. Box 2131
San Diego, CA 92112
(619) 234-4118

C.C.C. of Los Angeles
1300 W. Olympic Blvd. #304
Los Angeles, CA 90015
(213) 386-7601

C.C.C. of Orange County
1616 E.4th Street, Suite D
Santa Ana, CA 92701
(714) 547-8281

C.C.C. of Kern County
1706 Chester
Bakersfield, CA 93301
(805) 324-9628

C.C.C. of The East Bay
1212 Broadway, Suite 706
Oakland, CA 94612
(415) 832-7555

C.C.C. of Twin Cities
729 "D" Street
Marysville, CA 95901
(916) 743-1785

C.C.C. of Fresno
2135 Fresno St., Room 210
Fresno, CA 93721
(209) 233-6221

C.C.C. of Inland Empire
(San Bernardino)
3679 Arlington Ave., Suite E
Riverside, CA 92506
(714) 781-0114

C.C.C. of Pleasant Hill
(see The East Bay)

C.C.C. of Ventura County
3445 Telegraph Rd., $105
Ventura, CA 93003
(805) 644-1500

C.C.C. of Marin & Sonoma
  Counties
1371 Neotomas Ave, Suite A
Santa Rosa, CA 95405
(707) 527-9221

C.C.C. of Stockton
1325 N. Center St.
Stockton, CA 95202
(209) 464-8319

C.C.C. of North Valley
P.O. Box 4044
Redding, CA 96099
(916) 244-9626

D. Credit Fixit Groups

There are also a number of business organizations which advertise that for a fee they will improve or establish a good credit rating for you. Unlike C.C.C., many of these groups claim what amounts to magic powers to restore your credit rating, no matter what your credit history. In truth, most of these so-called "credit service" organizations provide little in the way of valuable services that you can't do for yourself after reading this book.

Think of it this way. If your credit history has been unfairly tarnished by the inclusion of debts you don't owe, or which you dispute, there are a number of state and federal laws which will help you clear up the problem (see Chapter 4 for "how to do it" information). On the other hand, if your credit rating is in terrible shape because you owe all sorts of people money, no credit fixit group will be able to magically convince people to lend you more money.

The problem of false ads claiming to be able to re-establish a good credit rating has gotten so bad that the California legislature has passed the Credit Services Act (C.C. 1789.10- 1789.23) to deal with it. This lengthy act provides that, among other things, any credit fixit business (except non-profit organizations) must:

* Engage in honest advertising and other business practices, especially when it comes to describing services and charges and handling a debtor's money;

* Not charge for referring a client to a lender who extends credit to a client on substantially the same terms as if the person was a member of the general public;

* Not council anyone to provide creditors with false or misleading information;

* Provide the client with a statement of their legal right to examine, and correct their credit file at any credit reporting agency (see Chapter 4);

* Provide the client with a written statement of their right to cancel the contract with the credit fixit agency within five days of signing it, along with a blank form for that purpose.

Anyone suffering damages as a result of violation of the Credit Services Act is eligible to sue for any actual damages suffered. Plus attorney fees and punitive damages. In no case will a victimized person be awarded less than the amount they paid the credit fixit group.

chapter 4

$ $ $ $ $ $

Credit Bureaus and Discrimination in Credit

Credit bureaus are a direct result of our insane credit system. The credit system expands because creditors thrust more and more credit into people's lives. But with each additional person using credit, the paranoia of the creditor in not collecting on the debt likewise increases. To protect themselves from their self-created paranoia, creditors keep intensifying their investigations of the people to whom they are lending money. The result--more credit bureaus. Sounds a bit crazy, huh.

A. What Are Credit Bureaus?

Credit bureaus are profit-making companies which are usually in partnership with collection agencies or are, in fact, collection agencies themselves. The bureaus survive by providing information on a person's credit reputation to other collection agencies, and to all kinds of creditors, like finance companies, department stores, car dealers, landlords, etc. If the bureau has no information on a person, it can't very well charge for providing a service. What that means is they're always out there digging.

Credit bureaus are known officially as Consumer Credit Reporting Agencies. There are also Investigative Consumer Reporting Agencies which report on your personal life. Most outfits are made up of both types of agencies, having all the information on you right on hand.

B. What Services Do They Provide?

It is the business of credit bureaus to gather as much data as possible on everyone, including you. With that information, they can provide their nasty service to any creditor who wants to know about you.

The frightening aspect of these bureaus is that they can gather information that goes beyond mere credit information. Under the law, they can collect data on your personal life, such as whether you are divorced, separated, have been arrested or convicted of a crime, or failed to pay a traffic fine. The law specifically provides for investigative information on your "general reputation," "personal characteristics" and "mode of living." Obviously these words could mean anything, and possibly they may only be limited by the imagination of the credit bureau people.*

Credit bureaus also keep "locate" lists. If, for example, ABC creditor has trouble finding Roger, who skipped out on one of their loans, they can give his name to the credit bureau and ask them to put his name on "locate." Then, each time a name is called in for some other reason, whether for a credit check by another creditor or perhaps by the person himself who wants to see his file, or whatever, it is checked against this list. If Roger's name comes up, they call ABC creditor and tell him that Roger has been found and has given 1 Blue Street, Pasadena, California, as his address. Pretty sneaky, don't you think?

C. How the Bureaus Work

Let's see what happens when someone-- let's call him Roger Owens--buys a car on credit.

Roger Owens goes to Trust-in-Man Autos and finds a 1980 Volvo with 80,000 original miles. He'd like to buy it and the salesman offers to sell it for the fine price of $1,000. Roger bites, and now the salesman needs to check his credit. For even though Roger must put $300 down, Trust-in-Man Autos must assure itself that Roger will be able to pay the remaining $700 plus interest at 15-18% a year.

The salesman calls Credit Bureau, Inc. (C.B.I.), one of the largest credit bureaus, to see what they have on Roger.** The person who answers will type on a computer terminal Roger's name, his social security number, his current address, former employment, his wife's name, her employment and perhaps also her social security number. All this information then appears before that person on the screen. The computer will digest the information and soon come up with a "file" on Roger. It will contain whatever credit information it has on him, including any bankruptcies within the last 10 years, law suits and judgments, tax liens, all within the last

---

* The "imagination" of credit bureau people often seems to tread on lawlessness. Instead of accurately checking sources on personal information it received, one of the largest credit bureaus in the country was recently found to be faking investigations and verifications. Even more outrageously, it bribed hospital employees, policemen, medical computer employees and anyone else it could in order to get official records of people for its files. All this was soundly illegal, not to say a ghastly invasion of privacy. See Petrocelli, William, LOW PROFILE, HOW TO AVOID THE PRIVACY INVADERS, 1981.

** Some bureaus are small and local, but others are national in scope. TRW, a credit and investigative reporting agency, for example, has offices from coast to coast and employs a small army of investigators.

18

seven years. If he's had trouble getting credit at another place, it may be written down here, as would any repayment difficulties he may have had. There is a rating system from 1 to 9, depending on whether he usually pays within 30 days (rating 1), 60 days (rating 2), 90 days (rating 3), etc., up to rating 8, where the item has been repossessed and rating 9 where the account is labelled "skip" and is referred for collection (see Chart).*

If all the information the salesman receives is sufficient for him, he will use it to make a decision as to whether Trust-in-Man Autos can "afford" to take the chance of financing Roger on the car.

Now, what if Roger recently moved here from Albuquerque? There may not be a record of him in the local credit bureau office. If that happens, the credit bureau will do two things. It will call its office in Albuquerque (if it has one) to see what they have on him. And it will start a new file on him, so if any other creditor needs to know about Roger, the bureau will be able to supply some information.

IMPORTANT: HOW LONG CAN A CREDIT BUREAU KEEP AN ITEM IN YOUR FILE? The credit bureau is permitted to keep the following credit information in your file (Civil Code Section 1785.13; 1786.18):

1. Bankruptcies which happened less than 10 years ago (see 15 U.S.C. Section 1681C).

2. Lawsuits and satisfied judgments which happened less than seven years ago.

3. Unsatisfied judgments which happened less than ten years ago.

4. Unlawful detainer (eviction) actions where the tenant loses the action.

---

* Rating systems and codes vary, but most are roughly like this example.

5. Any other adverse information which is less than seven years old.

6. Records of arrests and convictions up to seven years ago. However, if you were arrested but never convicted, the item must be removed immediately.

Consumer Credit Reports used in:

1. Credit transactions over $50,000;

2. Underwriting life insurance over $100,000;

3. Employment of an individual with an annual salary of $30,000;

4. Rental of a dwelling where the rent is over $1,000, may include adverse information which would otherwise be prohibited by the above rules.

Don't trust the credit bureau to automatically remove the information once the time period has passed. Review your file. Also, if the time period hasn't lapsed on an item, but you disagree with the way the information is presented in your file, you can dispute it [see H(3) below].

D. How to Keep Your Name out of Credit Bureaus

The above example should give you some clues on what to do if you don't want credit bureaus to have information about you. You see, the credit bureau finds you only when you find them. And you may find them each time you apply for credit, or loans, or employment, or even an apartment. Obviously, at some time you will have to rent a place or look for a job. But not every landlord or employer checks with a credit bureau. If possible, don't deal with people who want to do a check on you. For if the bureau has nothing on you when the creditor calls, it will start a file then. And, always pay in cash. You'll be happier in the long run and less paranoid.

Credit bureaus also find out about you if you file bankruptcy, or have lawsuits and judgments** brought against you. These facts surface because people from the bureau check local court records each week. But they usually only check local court records, so if you move to a new town, they won't necessarily know what your credit standing was before, unless you tell them.

E. What if You Have No File?

If the credit bureau has no file on you, some creditors might figure you're a good risk, especially if the reason there is no file is that you had no reason to get credit before. But most creditors will not figure you're a good risk, because you have not demonstrated that you can buy on credit and pay on time. To establish good credit, you might consider getting a department store credit card, purchasing a few small items, and paying for them as soon as you receive the bill. If you can't get a credit card any other way, you may succeed if you open an account at a savings and loan or bank which makes them available to depositors automatically.

F. Want to Know What Is in Your File?

Under California law, you have the right to see and copy your files. All you have to do is establish proper identification and usually pay a fee of up

** Credit bureaus will seldom include that you have paid the judgment or won the lawsuit.

to $8.00 (Civil Code Section 17, 1785.10, 1785.15, 1785.17k 1786.10, 1786.22, 1786.26).

G. Which Credit Bureau Should You Contact?

You can find a listing of credit bureaus in your area by looking up "Credit Reporting Agencies" in the yellow pages of your phone book.

There are often three or four credit bureaus in a locale, especially in major metropolitan areas. Some will be larger than others and one will probably contain more information on you than another. Among the largest in California are T.R.W., C.B.I. (Credit Bureau, Inc.), and Trans Union Credit.

Some bureaus may charge you less, or perhaps no fee at all, to see your file. If you are not afraid of giving your name to a credit bureau, call a few of them and see whether they have a file on you and if so, whether there is a charge for you to check it out.

Of course, if you've received a letter saying that your credit has been denied because of information in your file at a certain credit bureau, then that's where you will want to check. Under the law, if you were denied credit or you have been charged a greater than normal interest rate because of information in your file, you are permitted to see your file without charge if you ask to see it within 30 days. (The person who received the bureau report must tell you and give you the name of the bureau.)

H. After You've Found a Credit Bureau

1. Call the Bureau

Call the bureau and ask to see your file. They may establish your identity right then over the phone and tell you what's in your file. More likely, though, they'll either send you an identification form to fill out (and maybe give you a "code" number to use), or ask you to call back after they've searched for your file.*

If they want you to fill out a form, be careful. There are some bureaus that use their right to ask for identification to get even more information about you for their records. (After all, the more information they have on you, the more they will have to sell to collection agencies and creditors who want it.) Answer only those questions which will establish your identity, like your name, social security number, address and perhaps a previous address. One credit bureau asks for five years of previous addresses. There is usually no need to give them all that information. If a credit bureau refuses you the right to see your file after you provide "proper identification" and pay the fee, complain to one of the State Attorney General's offices listed at the end of this chapter.

In our experience, one bureau which reads files over the phone told us the day we called that the computer wasn't working and that we should call back. We did. And did. And did. And did. Each time all we got was a pleasant greeting and a hold. It took us three days to get back through to the woman with whom we were to discuss our file.

Another problem with calling by phone

is that if they do read your file over the phone to you, you can never be certain that they are telling you everything in it.

2. Seeing Your Computer Printout

Some offices will send you a computer printout of your file. Others will allow you to visit their offices to review the printout on the premises with a staff member. It doesn't really make that much difference, although if you review your statement in the company of a bureau employee, you can immediately receive clarification of all the unintelligible code numbers and symbols used. If you read it at home, you may find that the explanations printed on the bottom or reverse side of your statement are as indecipherable as the symbols they are interpreting. Calling up for clarification can be a bureaucratic nightmare.

If you visit the office, you are permitted to bring someone else with you. This is probably a good idea. Your friend can act as a witness if the bureau gives you any trouble in requiring you to fill out unnecessary forms, or makes you rush through the file, not giving you sufficient time to go over it carefully and ask questions.

The credit bureau must allow you to see all the information they have in your file (except medical information) at the time of your request, the sources of the information they have on you, the names of the people who have received information from your file within the last six months, and within the last two years if the information was given to an employer or potential employer of yours.

IMPORTANT: Don't let them skip over anything!

---

* A married or divorced woman can now use her birth given name and not have to refer to her husband or former husband's name to gain access to her file. See "B" of Part II of this chapter.

3. If You Disagree with Something in Your File

You have the right to dispute any item of information in your file. Bureaus very often have inaccurate or misleading material in their files. If you see something that isn't true or is inaccurate, complain. Under the law, the bureau is required to reinvestigate the matter. If you are right, or if the information can no longer be verified, the bureau must remove that information. Our experience has been that if you dispute an item, they'll often remove it or state it the way you feel it should be. Credit bureaus cannot afford the time and the staff to go out and recheck information on individual files.

If the bureau verifies the information and you still disagree with it, you are entitled to write a statement up to 100 words on the disagreement. The bureau people must include it in your file (Civil Code Section 1785.16, 1786.24).

a. Writing Your Statement

The law requires that the credit bureau people assist you with the writing of your statement if you ask them for their help. However, they may use pre-packaged statements or not help you say exactly what you want.

If you would rather write it yourself, ask the friend who has come with you to help. You can also wait until you get home to write it and bring it back another day.

We have provided below two different statements to give you an idea of how to write one.

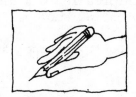

STATEMENT 1

Your records showing that I was not making payments on time to Rip-Off Furniture Store in Fresno are misleading. I stopped making payments to them only after the new sofa I purchased for $400 fell apart three months after I bought it. I decided that I would not pay any longer for such junk. After a few months went by, they contacted me and we settled the remainder of the account by my agreeing to give them only $50 more and to pay for the repair work myself. The account is closed and I owe them nothing.

Suzanne Porter

STATEMENT 2

Your records show that I am unemployed. That is incorrect. I am self-employed as a cabinet maker and carpenter. I work out of my home and take orders from people who are referred to me through various sources. My work is known in the community and that is how I earn my living.

Denny Porter

b. After a Change Is Made In Your File

If the bureau revises certain information in your file, or if you write a statement for inclusion in your file, the bureau must comply in the following manner: If you filed a statement, they must read your statement or give a summary of it to anyone to whom they give the report. The bureau must also notify any person who has received a report on you within 6 months (or 2 years if it involves employment) of the statement you have made, should you request the bureau to notify them. (There may be an additional charge for this.) BUT YOU HAVE TO DEMAND THAT IT BE DONE. You should also consider sending a copy of any such information to important creditors and others yourself, to be sure they receive it.

c. Preventive Tips

Applications for jobs, insurance, or apartments may spur investigative consumer reports, so be sure to correct any inaccuracies <u>before</u> making the application.

I. Complaints About the Credit Bureau

If you feel that the credit bureau or the person or creditor who received a report on you misused the report or otherwise failed to comply with the law, you should make a complaint to the State Attorney General's Office which covers your area. There is one in Sacramento,

San Francisco, Los Angeles, and San Diego. Their addresses and phone numbers are listed below. If you call these offices, they will send you a complaint form to fill out and return. If you would rather not call, you can send a letter which they will accept as a substitute for a complaint form. If you write a letter, include, if possible, the name of the company, its address, the name of the person you dealt with, the nature of the problem, any dates, and copies of any documents or letters that pertain to the problem. A sample letter follows.

Here is a list of Attorney General's Offices in the state. Contact the one nearest to you.

LOS ANGELES
Tishman Building
3580 Wilshire Blvd., Ste. 800
Los Angeles, CA 90010
(213) 736-2304

SAN FRANCISCO
350 McAllister, Rm. 6000
San Francisco, CA 94102
(415) 557-2544

SAN DIEGO
110 W. "A" Street, #700
San Diego, CA 92101
(619) 237-7351

SACRAMENTO
1515 "K" Street
Suite 511
Sacramento, CA 95814
(916) 322-3360

Toll free #s (within
California, but outside
Sacramento
(800) 952-5225
(800) 952-5548 (TYY machine
for hearing impaired *only*

615 Cloisters
San Diego, California
April 2, 19_

Consumer Complaint Division
State Attorney General's Office
110 W. "A" Street
San Diego, California 92101

Dear Sir:

I wish to make the following complaint concerning Sneaky Credit Bureau, 503 Grand Avenue, San Diego.

On March 29, 19_ I went down to Sneaky Credit Bureau to see my file. I paid $8.00 and waited until someone was available to help me. Finally, a Mrs. Jones came out and took me back with her to a small room. There she pulled out my file and started going through it.

However, she refused to show me certain pages, and when I asked her why, she said she didn't have to show these to me. She wouldn't tell me what kind of information was in it, but just ignored my question.

She also went through the file very quickly and wouldn't give me any time to stop and ask questions. When I asked her to check on a statement in the file that I felt was inaccurate, she told me not to worry about it.

Kindly investigate this matter and inform me of the results.

Very truly yours,

Georgeann Stewart

You can also contact your local District Attorney's Office if they have a consumer complaint division.

If the credit bureau is associated with a collection agency (and most of them are), you can also contact California Collection and Investigative Services, 1920 20th Street, Sacramento, CA 95814, (916) 739-3028

But probably, your best results will be with the Attorney General's Office.

If you were seriously screwed over by the credit bureau--for example, they repeatedly gave out false information on you after you corrected it--you may also want to see a lawyer. The law allows you to bring suit against credit bureaus in certain instances.

Under California law, you can sue credit bureaus for actual damages, including court costs, loss of wages, attorney's fees, and, when applicable, pain and suffering. In the case of a willful violation, you can recover punitive damages of $100 to $5,000 (Civil Code Section 1785.31). You can bring your case yourself in Small Claims Court (see Chapter 8).

J. Discrimination in Credit

The Federal Equal Credit Opportunity Act prohibits discrimination on the basis of race, color, religion, national origin, sex, marital status, age and being on public assistance. The law allows the creditor in certain circumstances to make limited inquiries on marital status, age and public assistance, but you cannot be denied credit or receive credit on less favorable terms merely because of these factors (15 U.S.C. Section 1691). California law also has some valuable protections (Civil Code Section 1812.30).

1. Sex and Marital Status

California law specifically guarantees equality of treatment in receiving credit to women and unmarried people.*

---

* In addition, the Federal Equal Credit Opportunity Act has been interpreted to prohibit credit discrimination against unmarried couples. This means the incomes of both members of an unmarried couple must be considered when they apply for credit to buy something jointly.

A woman, whether married or not, cannot be denied credit in her own name where a man having the same amount of earnings and other property would receive credit. Nor can she be offered credit on terms less favorable than a man in the same circumstances.

An unmarried person cannot be denied credit if a married person with the same amount of earnings and property would receive it. Neither can an unmarried person be offered credit on less favorable terms than those offered a married person in the same circumstances (Civil Code Section 1812.30).

Moreover, women (or men) who receive spousal and child support payments under a written agreement or court order may include these amounts in their "earnings." The bank can, however, check to make sure the payments are "reliable," i.e., that they have been regularly made and paid in full.

Pensions, social security, disability or survivorship benefits and other similar sources of income are also considered earnings.

2. Credit Bureau Files in Your Own Name

Credit bureaus must now file new credit information separately under the names of each person or spouse rather than under a joint account. A married or divorced woman can use her birth given name (or any other name) and not have to refer to her husband or former husband's name to gain access to her credit file [Civil Code Section 1812.30(e)].

If you are or were married and a credit bureau has you included in a joint credit file established before 1977, you can request either in writing or in person that the information be filed separately under both names (as is done with information since January 1, 1977) [Civil Code Section 1812.30(f)].

If you are thinking of ever obtaining credit, it is important that you request this change. This is because accounts of married people, even those opened in the names of both spouses, are often reported in only the husband's name. This has been generally true, regardless of who has been paying the bills or whose income was used to obtain the account. Thus many married women do not have a credit history in their own names, though their husbands do.*

3. If Action Is Taken on Your Credit and You're Not Satisfied

Federal and state law require that you are entitled to a statement of reasons explaining why, if: 1) you are denied credit; 2) you are refused credit in substantially the amount or the terms you requested; 3) there is a change in the terms of the credit arrangement you've had; or 4) your credit is revoked.

Some creditors provide this statement as a matter of course, but most do not. You are entitled to request the statement within 60 days after you have been notified of the creditor's decision. The creditor must then respond within 30 days after receiving your request. In most instances, you are entitled to a written statement if you make a written request for it. Otherwise, it may be

---

* You should definitely request that the change be made in the reporting of your credit history now. A divorced or widowed woman does not clearly have the same right to demand credit in the name of her former or deceased spouse as she does while she is still married.

oral (Civil Code Section 1787.2 and 15 U.S.C. Section 1691).

4. If You're Dissatisfied with the Treatment You've Received

If you feel that a bank or other creditor has discriminated against you or has not followed the law, you have a number of places to turn to for help.

Begin by contacting the state Attorney General's Office (see list above). Also, contact the Federal Trade Commission (F.T.C.). See Chapter 2.

Under state and federal law, you are entitled to your actual damages and punitive damages up to $10,000 plus attorneys' fees if you've been discriminated against. Contact an attorney. If you don't know any, see Chapter 3.

Unfortunately, although the law is clear on how banks and credit card companies can score a woman's credit, the reality is somewhat different. Banks still often ignore these laws as evidenced by the more than 10,000 complaints relating to credit discrimination received by the F.T.C. in a recent year. Various women's rights organizations, such as the Women's Credit Rights Project at the University of Southern California, report that only a few cases have been brought to court.*

---

* A federal appeals court has held that the American Express Company violated the federal law against discrimination based on marital status and sex by cancelling a woman's supplementary credit card upon the death of her husband, who was the primary cardholder. MILLER V. AMERICAN EXPRESS CO., 688 F.2d 1235 (1982).

$ $ $ $ $ $

chapter 5

Understanding Your Debts

A. Common Sense

There are as many ways of thinking about debts as there are people. However, before you can make any sensible headway, you must know where you are starting from. What is your income? How much do you owe, to whom and for what?

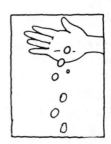

CHART 1: Start by finding out exactly what you take in each month from all sources:

Jobs   _____
Social Security   _____
Pensions   _____
Public Assistance   _____
Disability   _____
Other   _____

                  TOTAL   _____

CHART 2: Now list what it costs you to live each month (don't include any debt payments here except those necessary to that month, such as a car or mortgage payment).

Monthly Expenses

Food _____
Housing (rent, mortgage) _____
Medical Expenses _____
Property Taxes _____
Utilities _____
Telephone _____
Transportation (car payment
  repairs, public transit
  fees, gas) _____
Daily Expenses (lunch money,
  etc.) _____
Home Repair _____
Druggist _____
Dentist _____
Clothing _____
Church _____
Recreation _____
Other _____

                    TOTAL _____

CHART 3: Now list all of your overdue debts in their order of importance (you will want to read the rest of this chapter to understand the difference between secured and unsecured debts).*

	Mo. Payment	Amount Behind	Total Owed
Secured Debts			
Car (1)			
(2)			
Mortgage			
Finance Co. (1)			
(2)			
(3)			
Other (1)			
(2)			
(3)			
Unsecured Debts			
Child Support			
Hospital Bills			
Doctor (1)			
(2)			
(3)			
Dentist			
Credit Cards (1)			
(2)			
(3)			
Club Dues			
Dress Shop			
Hardware Store			
Department Store			
Record Club			
Attorney			

You may now find it helpful to make a mark next to each of your overdue debts--(X) for those that you consider it essential to pay, such as rent, utilities, child support, car payment, etc.;

* Interest is collectable on debts if it was called for in the original agreement between creditor and debtor. Collection agencies can continue to add on interest at the rate called for in the original sales agreement. Once a court judgment is entered, interest can only be charged at 10%.

(Y) for those which are somewhat less important, such as, perhaps, the dentist, doctor, and oil company; and (O) for those which aren't pressing at all, such as the health club, airlines, and department store. Of course, one of the items in the non-essential category may suddenly become more important if a creditor gets a judgment against you and threatens to attach your wages (see Chapters 9 and 10).

NOTE: The money you have available to pay overdue debts is that left over after you meet your essential monthly expenses (in Chart 2). If nothing is left over and you still have past due bills, you will want to think about the various strategies outlined in this book. Do not, under any circumstances, make payments on non-essential debts (such as the dress shop) when you have not paid for essential services.

IMPORTANT: You may think that this sort of advice is obvious, but it doesn't seem to be. We have seen so many sensible people panic when pressured by bill collectors and make payments on non-essential items only to face eviction because they can't pay the rent, or have their lights turned off because they let the utility bill slide.

Now we ask you to learn a little law. Whether you have had any legal training or not, it's important that you understand the difference between your secured and unsecured debts.

B. Difference Between Secured and Unsecured Debts

A debt is a debt is a debt, isn't that right? Well, not quite. There are two legal classifications of common debts and it's important that you understand the difference. It's not complicated and you can always flip back to this chapter if you have trouble keeping them straight.

1. Unsecured Debts [Most Common Debts]

If you borrow $500 from a friend, you are in debt. If you don't pay the debt, your friend can sue you in Small Claims Court, get a judgment and try to collect it. He could go after your wages, your bank account, or your property if he can find any which is not exempt under California law (see Chapters 10, 11 and 12). Obviously this whole procedure is fairly cumbersome and time consuming. You would have plenty of opportunity to protect yourself, while your friend would have to do quite a bit of work to get his money. Most debts operate this way and are called unsecured debts.

Unsecured debts include (this is not a complete list):

  a) doctor bills
  b) credit cards of all types
  c) store revolving charge accounts*
  d) loans with no collateral (whether from friends, banks, credit unions, etc.)
  e) attorney fees
  f) club dues
  g) utility bills**
  h) union dues**
  i) rent**

IMPORTANT: On unsecured debts the creditor has no right to the return of any merchandise or property. Thus, if you bought a dress, didn't pay for it, and then went bankrupt, you wouldn't have to return the dress.

---

* Be careful of this one. Most stores don't sell major items such as furniture and expensive appliances without getting a separate security agreement. See Section B2 of this chapter.

** While these debts are not secured, failure to pay them can result in immediate unpleasantness, such as being evicted, having the lights turned off, or losing your union membership.

2. Secured Debts

Now let's assume that your friend anticipated having trouble collecting the $500 and required that you pledge your stereo system as security for the loan, and got you to agree in writing that if the loan was not repaid within two months, he could take the stereo. After two months he could sue you, get a judgment, and instead of going through the complicated steps necessary to collect the money, could simply repossess the stereo to satisfy the debt.

Most debts in California are unsecured, but some specific types are usually secured. You have a secured debt when you have signed a contract (called a security agreement) which pledges some item of your property to be turned over to the creditor if you should fail to pay. Large expensive items are most likely to involve security agreements. If you buy large items such as furniture and major appliances, the seller will usually have you sign a security agreement. The same thing happens with new and used cars where the seller or lending institution keeps the pink slip until you make the last payment. A house mortgage involves exactly the same principle. If you fail to pay on any of these items, the creditor may quickly move to repossess or foreclose.*

UNSECURED DEBT IS ONE IN WHICH THERE IS NO SIGNED WRITTEN AGREEMENT.

SECURED DEBT IS ONE IN WHICH YOU SIGN A CONTRACT PLEDGING AN ITEM OF YOUR PROPERTY IF YOU FAIL TO PAY.

---

* Where furniture, appliances or other items of personal property are involved, the creditor would more likely elect to attach your wages. See Chapters 9 and 10.

In addition to the items mentioned above, you commonly have secured debts for boats, mobile homes, and snow mobiles. Many, but not all, loans from finance companies, banks, and credit unions are also secured. Security for these loans is often household furniture, or your car, if you have finished paying for it.

3. Differences in Collection

As we pointed out with the example of the stereo, it is much easier to collect on a secured than an unsecured debt. There are several reasons for this.

In one situation (motor vehicles, see Chapter 6), a secured item can simply be grabbed if you miss a payment. In other secured debt situations, the repossession of an item can follow directly from the judgment (see Chapters 9 and 11). On unsecured debts there is absolutely no right to take possession of the goods at any time.

The California exemption laws which allow a family to keep their house, car, furniture, etc. (see Chapter 11) don't protect you from a secured debt on the item itself. For example, if you bought a living room set on a sale contract that gave the seller the right to take the furniture if you didn't pay for it, you could not fail to pay and keep the furniture by claiming that it was exempt under the California law. Of course, whether you finished paying for the living room set or not, you would be protected by the exemption laws from having it taken and sold to satisfy any other debt, secured or unsecured. As you now know, if you got the living room set in the first place without a security agreement, you have no problem.

The same reasoning applies to all other secured debts. If you have a house, for example, filing a Declaration of Homestead (see Chapter 12) protects your equity from almost all debts, but it will not protect you from the holder of the mortgage. Thus, if you pay your mortgage, your doctor or the credit card company cannot touch your homesteaded house. However, if you pay the doctor and the credit card company but neglect the mortgage, the homestead won't help you.

Even in bankruptcy, there are differences between secured and unsecured debts. Bankruptcy will wipe out both, but with secured debts, you must return the item in question* to discharge the debts if they were incurred while purchasing the same property pledged as security. However, with ordinary unsecured debts and secured debts in which you pledged exempt household property (see Chapter 11) as collateral for a loan, and the purpose of the loan bore no relation to the property, you get to keep the goods and discharge the debt too. Don't get worried about this rule now, though. It's fully discussed in Chapter 18 and you will find that there are ways to keep secured property, such as your car and furniture, for far less than the original debt.

4. Effect of Returning Secured Item to Creditor

In many situations, the return of the secured item (couch, rug, TV, etc.) ends the obligation.* Thus, if you owe $500 on a TV and can't pay, the debt is wiped out if the TV is returned. There is a catch, however: the merchant or collection agency must be willing to accept the property. Being business people, they will usually do this only if they

think that the item or property is worth more in a resale transaction than the debt. Often a used and possibly damaged piece of furniture will be worth very little on resale. Under normal circumstances, for example, a finance company would prefer to try and collect a debt on a TV for $500 rather than take the TV back if it would sell for only $200. Their attitude would be much different, however, if a person were judgment proof or contemplating bankruptcy.

IMPORTANT: It is crucial that you know the difference between secured and unsecured debts. If you don't understand now, reread this chapter. It will probably be helpful to make a list of all your debts and identify which category each is in. Remember, you can get a copy of your contract from the creditor if you are in doubt as to its terms. As a general rule, it is better to pay secured debts before unsecured debts if you want to keep the secured item.

5. Debts and Divorce

The whole area of community and separate property and community and separate debts is discussed in detail in CALIFORNIA MARRIAGE AND DIVORCE LAW, Warner and Ihara, Nolo Press. Problems most commonly develop when a judge orders one spouse to pay certain debts and that person fails to do so. The creditor then proceeds against the other spouse, who normally feels very put upon, because under the divorce order, the debts aren't his or her responsibility.

The law unfortunately is simple. Both spouses are still on the hook to the creditor no matter what the divorce decree says and the creditor can proceed against either. If the spouse who was not ordered to pay under the divorce decree ends up paying the creditor, that spouse does have a legal right to recover from the other spouse. Unfortunately, as we learn throughout this book, having a legal right and being able to enforce it aren't always the same thing.

---

* Actually, you have three choices: 1) you can accept the creditor's estimate of value of the item, pay the amount, and keep the property; 2) decide to let the creditor repossess; or 3) disagree with the creditor's estimate of value, but retain the property by making a deal.

* This rule does not apply to banks and finance companies, which advance money and take security in return. Also, it does not apply to any motor vehicle. See Chapter 6.

chapter 6

$ $ $ $ $ $

Repossession Before Court Action— Motor Vehicles

A. It's Mostly Illegal

Until a few years ago your wages, bank account, and property could be taken from you <u>without</u> a court decision that your creditor was entitled to them. It's hardly believable, but true nevertheless. This sort of thing was legal because finance companies, collection agencies, banking associations, and retailers spent a lot of money on political campaigns and lobbyists to see that the legislature did nothing to threaten their profits. It has only been in the last generation that a series of court decisions has resulted in an almost universal rule that it is unconstitutional to take wages or property from a person before he has his day in court.

Today no one can take your wages or bank account without going to court and getting a judgment against you (see Chapters 9 and 10) with the exception of the state and federal governments enforcing claims for unpaid taxes (see Chapter 16). Similarly, no one can enter your home and take any item of your property without first suing you, getting a judgment and then turning the judgment over to the sheriff or marshal (see Chapters 8 and 9). The fact that you owe money on an item secured by a contract which says they can enter and take the item if you fall behind in payments makes no difference. This sort of contract provision is no longer enforceable.

Of course, a creditor may try to talk you into voluntarily returning a piece of property. You may wish to do this because, as we have mentioned in Chapter 5, in many situations your entire debt is cancelled when the secured item is returned, or you may want to avoid being sued and having court costs and attorney fees added to the judgment. There is, however, absolutely no requirement that you return any item voluntarily, no matter how many payments you have missed. (If you are judgment proof--see Chapter 1--you may want to keep the goods as long as possible, since the amount of the judgment may be of little importance to you.) Don't let anyone threaten you into doing anything you don't want to do. No one can send a truck to your home to get your furniture or send the police out because you have missed a payment. If you receive a threat, complain to California Collection and Investigative Services, 1920 20th Street, Sacramento, CA 95814, (916) 739-3028.

B. Motor Vehicle Repossessions

Motor vehicles (cars, trucks, and motorcycles, but not mobile homes* or boats) and motor vehicle financing is huge business with huge profits. At every level of our society, people in this business are used to getting their own way. Bill collecting is no exception. Most things that we have set forth about the rules that protect the consumer from unfair collection practices do not apply to motor vehicles. Motor vehicles can be repossessed without a law suit even having been filed. In fact, they can be repossessed if you

---

* Those mobile homes which are stationary and need not be licensed under the Vehicle Code are exempt from the special strict deficiency judgment and prejudgment repossession rules discussed in this chapter. However, motor homes which must be licensed are treated like cars, trucks and motorcycles and are subject to the repossession and deficiency judgment rules discussed here. See Civil Code Section 1802.1 Also see Chapter 11(b) where we discuss exemptions from attachments for housetrailers and mobile homes you reside in.

miss a payment by one day. All the creditor has to do is go out and take the vehicle. You need not even be notified before they take it. As cutthroat as it sounds, it's also perfectly legal.

In practice, it's unlikely that a vehicle would be picked up because a payment is a day or two late, but we have seen it happen where a finance company or bank learns some facts that convince them that a person's credit situation has gotten much worse. This might happen if a wife calls up the finance company to say that she has left her husband because he has lost his job and been arrested. Normally the legal owner (the person who has the pink slip) will call you or write a letter or two before they come after the vehicle. Still, if you are going to have to be a little late with your payment, it's a wise idea to call the lender to let them know what's happening. In most cases, especially if you have a decent past record and appear to be sincere, they will work with you rather than pick up the car. After all, the bank is in the money business, not the used car business. A little caution is always sensible, however--don't tell them where the car is until you reach an understanding.

Finance companies are the most likely to grab a motor vehicle as soon as a payment is missed. Banks are a little less likely to move quickly and credit unions are fairly patient. When the decision is made to pick up a vehicle, the debtor is not notified. The creditor hires a person who specializes in legally "stealing" cars, and supplies the debtor's address, place of business, etc. The repossessor then hunts for the vehicle. Often he will find it sitting in front of the debtor's house or in the driveway. He will then wait until the debtor is asleep, call the police to tell them what he is doing, and then, using a master key, if possible, or hot wiring if not, simply drive off. If the vehicle is in a locked garage, the re-possessor can not legally break in to get it, as this would leave him open to be sued. Some repossessors will take a vehicle from an unlocked garage when they only have to open the door, and some will not. They will all grab a vehicle in the driveway or under a car-port.

If the vehicle is not near the house, a search will be made in the neighbor-hood. Most people who think that their car, truck, or motorcycle may be repos-sessed will make some effort to hide it. They won't go to too much trouble, how-ever, as that would cancel out the con-venience of having the vehicle in the first place. Many times people park a car about three blocks from their home when they fear repossession, far enough away to be hard to find, but close enough to still be convenient. The repossessors have long since learned this little bit of psychology, however, and often find the vehicle within min-utes after the start of the search. Leaving the motor vehicle in the locked garage of a neighbor is probably the best way to protect it.*

IMPORTANT: No one has the right to take a motor vehicle from your personal possession without your consent. If anyone tries to take the vehicle while you are present, they are liable for any harm done you or the property that is reasonably related to their actions. You have the right to protect yourself and the motor vehicle without liability to yourself, but you can not start any hostile or violent behavior if none is used against you.

---

* A dealer might argue that you were concealing the car in order to avoid repossession. If the judge goes along with his position, you would lose the right to reinstate the contract. Civil Code Section 2983.2. (See Section C, below.)

C. Getting Your Motor Vehicle Back

When a vehicle is legally repos-sessed, your right to possess it under the sales contract and security agree-ment is temporarily wiped out, and under the contract the creditor will sell it unless you are able to 1) reinstate the contract, or 2) redeem the contract.

1. Reinstatement

After repossession, California law* provides the debtor the right to rein-state the sales contract and security agreement on the same terms once in any twelve-month period (but only twice over the term of the contract). If your car is repossessed twice in one year, for example, you will not have the right to reinstate the contract the second time. Similarly, if your car is repossessed a third time under the same contract, you are not eligible for reinstatement.

EXCEPTIONS

As is true with most legal protec-tions there are exceptions to reinstate-ment rights. The seller does not have to reinstate if he/she determines in good faith that:

■The buyer provided false or mis-leading information on his or her credit application;

■The buyer concealed or removed the car from the state to avoid repposses-sion; or

■The buyer has failed to take care of the car and it has, or may, become substantially reduced in value (Civil Code Section 2983.3).

** Cal. Civil Code Sections 2983.2 and 2983.3 or Financial Code Sections 22465 and 24465, depending on who the creditor is.

Although you can argue that the misinformation on your credit application was the result of an honest error and not of material importance anyway, or that you were parked in your neighbor's garage because it is cleaner, larger, more convenient, etc., or that you did in fact take reasonable care of your car, it is pretty clear that these exceptions are so broad that they don't offer much protection. Nevertheless, the law does state that the seller must bear the burden of proof in justifying his refusal to reinstate the contract.

In the event of reinstatement, the buyer must make all payments in arrears, as well as any applicable delinquency charges. The buyer is also required to reimburse the seller for all reasonable and necessary collection and repossession costs and fees, including attorneys' fees and expenses related to the retaking and holding of the car. These incidental fees can sometimes be breathtakingly high, but you generally have little choice but to pay them if you wish to reinstate.

If the repossession occurred because you failed to maintain mandatory insurance on the car, you may be required to obtain insurance, or reimburse the creditor if he/she has taken out the insurance, before you will be allowed to reinstate.

To avail yourself of this remedy, you should contact the creditor as soon as possible and work out the terms. If you don't seize the initiative, either because you're in shock or are broke, here is what will happen next.

NOTE: If the seller fails to provide proper notice to the debtor of his or her right to reinstate the contract, or otherwise interferes with the debtor's reinstatement right, the creditor may be liable to the debtor for the entire value of the car, as well as punitive damages. CERRA V. BLACKSTONE, 172 Cal.App.3d 604 (1985).

Within 60 days of the repossession, the creditor is required to give you, and any co-signers on the contract, a 15-day Notice of Intent to Sell, which must either be handed to you or sent by certified mail, return receipt requested, to your addresses as shown on the contract (unless a change of address has been filed with the creditor, of course).

The Notice of Intent to Sell must provide a full and accurate accounting of all money paid and owed and give you 15 days (20 if you live outside of California) to either reinstate the contract or "redeem" the car. If you don't, or can't opt for the reinstatement remedy, you must pay the full amount of the contract balance within 15 days to get the car back. If you request it, the creditor must extend the redemption period for an additional 10 days. If you don't redeem or reinstate within the period allowed, the car will be sold.*

2. Personal Property in Repossessed Motor Vehicles

You are entitled to the return of all personal property (i.e., books, clothes, tools, sporting equipment, etc.) left in a car that is repossessed. You are not entitled to the return of anything related to the car, such as a spare tire or car radio. Simply contact the creditor and ask that your property be returned. They will normally be cooperative. If they are not, see a lawyer or consider bringing a suit in Small Claims Court.

D. Automobile Deficiency Judgments

You probably won't believe this one, so brace yourself. After the motor vehicle is repossessed, the creditor can turn around and sell it wholesale at a

---

* Cal. Civil Code Section 2983.2.

car auction or to a used car lot for far less than its retail value and sue you for the difference between what you still owe on the contract and what he sold the vehicle for. For example: You agreed to pay $4,000 for a car, paid $800 down and then another $1,200 in payments before you lost your job and missed several payments. The balance owed on the contract is $2,000. The car can then be repossessed and sold wholesale. Assuming the car could be sold retail for $2,000 with a newspaper ad, it might bring $1,200 wholesale to a used car lot, perhaps less, as wholesale auto sales in this situation are notoriously dishonest. You would then be sued and would find yourself with a "deficiency" judgment against you for $800 (the difference between the $2,000 you owed at the time of repossession and the $1,200 that the creditor sold the car for), plus repossession costs, sales costs and legal fees. It stinks, doesn't it? Well, it doesn't smell much better when the money is being passed around the state capitol to keep the law on the books. Every consumer organization in the state has supported legislation to do away with motor vehicle "deficiency" judgments, with no success. It has been getting closer in recent years, but the auto lobby still seems to have more bucks than consumers have votes. Little people are still paying thousands in car payments, losing their cars, and getting nailed with huge judgments.

Fortunately there has been some effort to reform the deficiency judgment mess. Thus, Section 2983.8 of the Civil Code states that there can be no deficiency judgment unless the sale of the motor vehicle was in conformity with Division 9 of the commercial code, including Section 9504.* Practically, this means the vehicle must have been disposed of in a "commercially reason-

able" manner. Unfortunately, "commercially reasonable" is defined in extremely vague language, with one exception. The debtor must be given written notice as to the time and place of the sale. Notice must be mailed five days before the sale to the debtor's address, as set out on the security agreement, or to any other address the debtor has furnished. Notice shall also be published in a newspaper.

What all this amounts to is this. If you have any doubt as to the fairness of the sale (and you probably should), show up and check it out. If you feel the vehicle was sold for far too little, or the sale was rigged, demand a court hearing when you are notified of the deficiency judgment proceeding. Be prepared to show up in court with proof that the sale was not "commercially reasonable." Wholesale prices paid for a comparable vehicle at about the same time should help.

E. Motor Vehicle Repair Laws

A person who repairs a car or motorcycle (mobile homes which don't need to be registered are not included) is entitled to be paid for labor and materials when the car is picked up, as long as the repairs are made for a dollar amount authorized by the vehicle owner. If a written statement of charges for completed work is presented to the owner and the owner does not pay, California law entitles the repair person to initiate proceedings to sell the vehicle.

If the vehicle has a value of between $100 and $1,000, according to Section 3072 of the Civil Code, it may be sold by the mechanic to satisfy the bill, so long as formal "lien proceedings" are begun within 15 days of the date the car is withheld. These proceedings require you to be given notice of the intended sale, an opportunity to file a Declaration of Opposition, and your day in

---

* There are no deficiency judgments on mobile homes unless they are substantially damaged. Civil Code Section 2983.8.

court to tell your side of the story, assuming that you've mailed your Declaration of Opposition to the Department of Motor Vehicles within 15 days of the date the Notice of Pending Lien Sale form was mailed to you. For more information on these proceedings, take a look at Civil Code Section 3072.

If your vehicle is worth more than $1,000, and the bill is not paid within 30 days of the time the work is completed, the mechanic must apply to the Department of Motor Vehicles for authorization to sell. If the mechanic's application is in order, the Department will send you a notice of pending sale, a blank Declaration of Opposition form, and information about your right to be heard in court. If you send the Declaration of Opposition form back to the department within 15 days of the date it was mailed to you, the mechanic will be informed by the Department that the vehicle cannot be sold without a court judgment or a release from you being obtained. Again, for more detail on how this procedure works, see Civil Code Section 3072.

There are additional technical requirements for sale of a car under this procedure which have not been covered here, but which must be satisfied for a legal sale. The group of statutes covering this subject begin at Civil Code Section 3067.1, and if you can find an irregularity in the procedures used by the mechanic, you may have a claim against him or be able to get your car back.

If the vehicle is sold, the proceeds of the sale are applied to pay off the repair bill, storage costs and actual selling costs (not to exceed $50). The balance is forwarded to the Department of Motor Vehicles and the legal owner then files a claim requesting the balance. The DMV does not have to honor claims which are filed more than three years after the sale.

At any time before the sale, the owner may get her vehicle back by paying the repair bill plus the storage costs and the actual costs incurred in sale preparations (not to exceed $50). After the sale, the legal owner may redeem a car worth more than $1,000 by paying the amount of sale, plus all costs and interests of the sale, together with 12% interest. This must be done within 10 days after the sale and does not apply to vehicles worth less than $1,000 [see Cal. Civil Code 3071].

In any event, any portion of a bill for repair work or services which is in excess of $750, or storage in excess of $400 ($500 if the car is worth more than $1,000 and an application for a lien sale has been filed) is invalid unless the repair or storage person has given actual notice in writing to the legal owner and has obtained his consent *before* beginning the repairs or storage.*

IMPORTANT: If you get into a dispute with a repair person over motor vehicle repairs, it is wise to get your car back first and argue later. We know of people who, after concluding that they were being cheated, paid the garage by check and then stopped payment on the check after they got the car back. This sort of approach is liable to result in the repair person starting a lawsuit against you and could even involve criminal "bad check" charges. A more moderate course would be to complain to the State of California Bureau of Automobile Repair, which is listed in all metropolitan phone books. Still another possibility, if the bill is over $50, is to pay it with a credit card and then argue about it later with the credit card company. This procedure is discussed in detail in Chapter 14, Section D. Also, don't forget Small Claims Court.

---

* Civil Code Section 3068.

chapter 7

$ $ $ $ $ $

How to Deal With Bill Collectors*

Bill collecting is big business, and just like any other big business, the idea is to make as much money as possible. This means that lots of people like you are going to have to cough up lots of cash. How you should respond to bill collectors depends upon what you want from them. You may want extra time to pay. Or to lower the size of your payments. Or not to pay at all. Whatever your objective, always keep this in mind: BILL COLLECTORS WORK ON THE PSYCHOLOGY OF FEAR. If they have you scared, they have you. As you will find out by reading this chapter, there is really not much they can do to you. If

you're afraid, you'll do a lot worse to yourself than they can ever do. So decide on your best course of action and be firm about it. If you stick to your guns and don't panic, you will be able to take those sensible steps necessary to take care of your debts and sleep well in the process.

A. When Bills Start to Pile up

One day the mail arrives and there are several letters from companies with which you have accounts suggesting politely that perhaps you have overlooked their last bill. If it's convenient,

---

* We are often asked if, once a bill is turned over to a collection agency, interest is still collectable. The answer is yes. If interest was called for on the original debt, the collection agency can keep adding it on at the same rate until a court judgment is entered, at which time the interest rate becomes 10%. See Chapter 8.

they would appreciate your paying it. This, of course, is a form letter that goes out automatically on every account that is overdue. If you fail to respond to the first letter, there will be more. Most companies send out their notices by computer. The computer, in effect, holds a package of these notices and merely sends out one after another, waiting a certain period of time between mailings. Each notice is a little stiffer and more threatening than the last, until finally you will be told that if you don't pay immediately, your account will be turned over to an attorney for legal action. This is nonsense. The creditor will give the account to a collection agency which will take <u>at least</u> several months to start a law suit.

The content of the letters varies from company to company. Some remind you of how valuable your credit rating is, while others spend more time trying to convince you of the wretchedness of law suits, wage attachments, and repossessions. Some companies will phone you one or more times to ask you when they can expect a payment, some will not.

Most large companies, such as department stores, gasoline retailers, and clothing stores, have small collection departments. These are the people who send the first few letters. Normally they do not get heavy, and rarely resort to harassment because they believe it's bad for their public image to be identified as hard-hearted scrooge types. There are also favorable tax laws which allow the company to deduct the value of the merchandise from their income, resulting in very little out-of-pocket loss. After several form letters and a phone call or two fail to get you to pay, they will turn the account over to an independent collection agency. Of course, a month or two after your first payment is overdue, they will cancel your credit privileges.

1. Need More Time to Pay?

Often when the first notices of overdue accounts arrive you will want to pay the bills, but will be temporarily short of funds. All you need is a little extension of time from your creditors. Your best bet is to ask for it directly and politely. Write a letter to all of your overdue accounts and explain what the problem is and when they may expect you to catch up on your payments. If you can send a partial payment, this will be helpful, but it is not absolutely necessary. Even a token payment of $10 or $20 tends to be some indication of good faith. You might write something along the lines of the letter that follows.

---

45 Ayse Street
San Leandro, California
May 12, 19__

Honorable Al's Toggery
100 Broadway
Oakland, California

Dear Sirs:

I just received your notice that I am overdue in paying my account. I am very concerned about this and have failed to pay only because several family emergencies have prevented me from doing so. These include [being laid off, sick, disabled, unexpected tax obligation, illness to family member, or whatever other excuses you have or can think up].*

My financial situation will improve in the near future. [Mention any particularly promising facts, such as returning to work, getting a raise, getting a workers' compensation award, selling property, etc.] I expect to be able to pay you on August 15, 19__.

I will appreciate any consideration you can give me. Should you wish to discuss this matter, please feel free to call me at 765-4321 in the evening.**

Very truly yours,

Zeynep Kora

---

* One common reason for failure to pay bills is divorce or separation. In this situation, there is rarely enough money to maintain two households. Creditors know this and get very nervous when they hear of a divorce or separation, so as a general rule, it's better not to list this reason.
** Don't put down a work phone number unless the creditor already knows where you work.

CAUTION: This approach works a lot better with the original creditor than it does with a collection agency. Professional bill collectors often view reasonableness as weakness (see B, below).

If you fail to pacify the creditor, or believe that circumstances require a little more clout, you might consider visiting a lawyer and having him or her write the letter to your creditors (see Chapter 3). The lawyer will not say anything much different than you would, but his stationery alone will guarantee that more respect is given the letter. The creditor knows, too, that if he doesn't cooperate with the lawyer's request for more time, the lawyer is likely to recommend bankruptcy.

IMPORTANT: In reading letters or taking phone calls from creditors, do not allow yourself to be scared or intimidated into any unwise actions. After reading this book you should have a clear idea of your situation and how to handle it. Don't alter your plan without good reason. If you have decided that your first priority is your home payment, your second priority is buying food and your third is your car payment, don't allow the dress shop to talk you into sending them $50 unless the important items have been taken care of.

REMINDER: Anxiety is your worst enemy and your creditor's main weapon. Relax, enjoy your supper, and keep the bills in perspective. Some of the wisest, finest people in history were late on their bills. Who really cares that Mark Twain was always in debt. We remember him for his beautiful works, not for his fiscal problems with the butcher. Only you can make yourself anxious and miserable. Your creditors will do everything in their power to encourage these feelings, but they have no real power.

B. How Collection Agencies Operate

This is the guts of the bill collection process. Sooner or later most unpaid bills, whatever the source, are turned over to collection agencies.* If you take a little time to understand how these agencies work, you will be way ahead when you deal with them. Some of the information contained in this section also applies to company bill collections, but is put here because it is most often used by collection agencies.

Most people in most collection agencies are paid to be nasty, brutal, and to hang on to you like a blood-thirsty tick. Occasionally you find someone with a little human understanding in this business, but don't count on it. Most collectors work on the theory that if you are harassed often enough, you will get some money up somehow. There are tens of thousands of collection agencies in this country and many of them are very prosperous, so you can see that these tactics work.

Collection agencies are private business operations which specialize in collecting overdue accounts. They usually take the accounts from the original creditor (store, doctor, credit union, etc.) with the understanding that they receive a percentage of any money recovered, with the rest going back to the creditor. The percentage the collection agency gets varies, usually depending on how easy the debt is to collect.

---

* On occasion, businesses will fake turning accounts over to collection agencies. They simply buy forms with a phony collection agency name on top and send them out themselves. If you get a letter from a collection agency, look in the phone book to see if they really exist. A variation of this scheme is a collection agency which offers creditors a series of dun letters, with little or no other collection activity except listing the debtor as a bad credit risk. The theory of this sort of collection effort--which is particularly likely to be used for small bills such as magazine subscriptions, doctor bills, etc.--is that lots of people will pay if they receive a series of dun letters, but if they don't pay, it's simply too expensive to sue.

A collection agency will have a relatively easy time collecting overdue accounts forwarded by reputable stores and well-managed credit unions where careful credit checks are made before credit is extended. The debtor will probably be fairly easy to locate, capable of working, and not particularly hostile to the original creditor. One-third of the amount recovered would be a typical collection agency fee for this type of account. However, a collection agency trying to collect the accounts of a credit jeweler with a dubious reputation for honesty, a health spa, or a cut-rate meat outfit would certainly demand a higher percentage, probably at least fifty percent of the original debt and perhaps more. Sometimes a collection agency will simply purchase old debts from the creditor and try to collect more than the price they paid for the debt. This is unusual. The percentage method is the one normally used.

Collection agencies have their own bureaucracy. They operate on a volume basis. At any one time they have thousands of accounts (some of the big ones have tens of thousands). On most of these, they will recover little or nothing, often because they simply can't locate the debtors. Collectors operate by trying to distinguish those accounts where success looks likely from those where it does not, and then going after the former full speed ahead.

When you receive a dun letter after the original debtor has given up, you can be sure that it's from a professional collector. Don't be misled by such names as Central Adjustment Service, Associated Credit Bureau, or Bureau of Medical Economics. You are only dealing with a collection agency. Don't take letters on legal stationery too seriously. Collection agencies have close working relationships with attorneys and commonly send out hundreds of form letters over the attorney's rubber-stamped signature, hoping to scare you. The attorney usually never sees the actual letters; they are sent directly from the collection agency's office. In many cases, no lawsuit is actually filed. It's cheap to threaten, expensive to sue. Some collection agencies never file lawsuits, especially for small bills (i.e., anything under $200-$300).*

1. They Can't Hurt You if They Can't Find You

There are lots of reasons why you may have no desire to negotiate a settlement. Perhaps you have so many debts that only bankruptcy makes sense (see Chapter 18), or you may be judgment proof (see Chapter 1), or you may not want to pay for any number of other reasons.

Whatever your situation, remember collection agencies or other creditors can't sue you, take your wages, harass you by mail or phone, or otherwise bother you if they can't locate you. People move a lot these days and often change jobs. Many times a debtor can't be located by the time an account has

---

* It is a violation of the Fair Debt Collection Practices Law for a creditor to falsely threaten to sue. He can be liable for your actual damages and for a penalty of $100-$1000.

been turned over for collection. Moving a long distance is a particularly good way to avoid a creditor. This is because collection agencies are local and are simply not organized to collect debts out of state.* There is a procedure by which a collection agency in one part of the country can assign a debt or judgment to a collection agency located at the place where you have moved, but forwarded debts do not receive the same time and attention as do local ones. The commission in these cases must be split between two collection agencies, making this type of collection far less profitable. In addition, a collection agency half way across the country from the original creditor can expect little if any repeat business and has no incentive to put much effort into a difficult collection.

NOTE: When dealing with a collection agency located far from the creditor, you can gain breathing space by raising several questions about the debt. For example, you might question the accuracy of the balance claimed to be owed, or state that you never received one of the items in question. Before proceeding, the agency will have to check out the questions with the forwarding collection agency which in turn will have to check with the original creditor. This often slows things down several months.

When a collection agency gets an account, they also get all the information that the original creditor has about you. This will include your address, phone, place of work, bank, car registration number and whatever else appeared on the original credit application. The collection agency will first try to write or call you. Often they use the certified letter, registered letter, or telegram ploy. They hope you will sign for one of these, thereby telling the agency where you are.

If you have moved, the agency will check the post office for a forwarding address and will of course examine the phone books for the greater metropolitan area. Should this fail, the next step is to call your job, with the collector posing as a friend or business associate. If you have changed jobs, the collector will often pretend to be a long lost friend or relative and try to worm your new location out of an unsuspecting friend. They have a lot of experience at this and are often totally convincing. Another common strategy is to try and get the personnel department to give them the address to which they sent your W-2 tax forms. Again, the collector poses as a friend of yours.

If the above fails, the next step is to contact the Department of Motor Vehicles to see if you have informed them of your new address. Collectors can get this information for $2.00 and are presently, through the state association of collection agencies, fighting all proposed legislation aimed at making D.M.V. information confidential.** Another tactic often used is to check with the Registrar of Voters in the county of your last residence. If you have reregistered in the county, the registrar will have your new address.

Also, the collector is likely to check the criss-cross, or street address

---

* There are several "national" collection agencies--Equifax, TRW, etc.--but even they are nowhere near as efficient at tracking debtors around the country as they would like to have you believe.

** The DMV now requires the person making the request to have a legitimate reason for requesting the information (e.g., hit-and-run accident, debt, unpaid judgment, etc.). The person must identify him/herself and verify the identification. As soon as the person receives the information, you must be notified as to what information was provided and to whom it was provided. A record of all this is kept at the DMV. Professional bill collectors may qualify to get information without the need to provide specific information with each request. Civil Code Section 1798.26.

phone directory published by the phone company. This will tell him the names and phone numbers of your near neighbors. By calling neighbors and posing as a friend, it's often possible to find out where you have moved, especially if you haven't warned the neighbors. Unlisted numbers and numbers where no address is listed don't appear in the criss-cross directory. Also, utilities such as the electric company may have a new address if you have moved within their service area, but several collectors indicate that this information is hard to get.

Most collection agencies will not do a great deal more beyond listing the debtor's name with the local credit bureau on the locate list.* In some cases, they may try to contact friends or relations listed on the original credit applicaton, but they won't push the search too hard.** It is not profitable for them to do so. They make their money from the large number of cases where they can find people fairly easily, not by extended man hunts for missing persons.

NOTE: Creditors can't legally get your location from Social Security, Veterans, State Unemployment, Disability or Welfare Department records. This information is supposed to be confidential. There have been a few cases where government employees with access to the computerized records have been paid off. A collector friend tells us that the risk is too high in trying to get information from these sources and that he believes it is almost never done.

▼

* This means that if you apply for credit in the same geographical area, the collection agency will promptly be told of your whereabouts. See Chapter 4.

** One other technique is to check with the County Assessor's Office to find out who owns the house you moved out of--the collector then calls the landlord and tries to get your forwarding address.

2. Negotiating a Settlement

By this point you should have a good grasp of your situation, including the difference between your secured and unsecured debts (see Chapter 5). If you are working or have some valuable property (such as land) that a creditor could grab, you should be particularly concerned to take defensive action before the collection agency draws blood. Remember, if you have not yet been sued (see Chapter 8) and your auto (see Chapter 6) and your home (see Chapter 12) are protected, you have some breathing space. Your wages, bank account, and other property can't be taken until after a judgment has been entered in court, except for tax obligations (see Chapter 16). This can't occur until after you have been sued and have been served with legal papers (see Chapter 8).

Collection agencies commonly accept cash settlements far below the full amount of the debt to avoid spending months trying to collect the whole thing. There is no rule as to how much they will accept to give you a complete release. We recommend an initial offer of about one-third of the original debt amount for bargaining purposes. This is probably a little low, although we have seen a number of debts settled at this level, where the agency believes that collection would be difficult or impossible in any other way. Settlement for 40 to 60 percent of the debt is more normal, but it's always wise to start a little low. Full cash payment of the compromise amount (or at least a large initial payment) is almost always a condition to this sort of arrangement.

A collection agency clearly has a strong motive for accepting $250 on a $500 debt if they get the money in cash. They close their books, take their percentage and forget about you. There is little reason, however, for the agency to reduce the debt total if you offer payments. They still have to keep track of you and always face the possibility that after a payment or two, you will again stop paying.

In negotiating, paint a bleak picture of your financial circumstances. Be sure to go into detail about illnesses, depressions, problems with work, etc. Most people have plenty of reasons why their bills cannot be paid in full. Of course, mentioning that you are seriously considering bankruptcy is always a good idea. Never tell a collection agency where you live, work, bank or can be reached if they don't already know. Never send in a payment by a check from your bank. Use money orders and buy them at a place other than where you bank. If a collector asks for personal information, tell him simply and politely that the information is none of his business.

IMPORTANT: It is wise to contact a collection agency if, and only if, you decide to seriously negotiate. If you can't lay your hands on enough cash to make a realistic offer, don't call them. Your contact may be the very thing that lets the agency know your location. They send out thousands of form letters a month. A large number of these never connect with the debtor, so the fact that you have received a letter doesn't mean that they know where you are.

You might want to think about having a lawyer help you with your negotiating.

This, of course, isn't necessary, and lots of people do splendidly on their own. But following the same reasoning mentioned in Section A of this chapter, the attorney, just by being an attorney, commands more respect than you do. Of course, this is a silly way to run the world, but it's still true. Also, an attorney has negotiated hundreds of similar cases and should have a pretty good intuition as to the best settlement possible in your situation. Again, remember, mention of bankruptcy by an attorney carries considerably more clout than does your mention of it. A nice side benefit of involving a lawyer is the California law prohibiting a collection agency from contacting you directly once they know you have an attorney. If they do, complain to the State at once. But, if you get a lawyer, be sure you know in advance what the lawyer will do and exactly what it will cost.

a. Secured Debts

The fact that a debt is secured by an agreement stating that if the debt is not paid, some item must be returned (such as furniture) doesn't change the basic strategy discussed above, but it does add another bargaining chip to the game. For discussion, let's assume you borrowed $1,500 from your credit union and pledged your living room set as security. A divorce has left you no money and a pile of debts, and this particular debt has been assigned to Blackbeard Bloodhound's Collection Agency. The furniture is pretty well worn, a few pieces have been junked, and you and your former wife have divided the rest, which taken together is worth about $350.

When the people at Blackbeard Bloodhound's contact you, they are sure to threaten to take the furniture. As you know, they can't do this unless you give it to them voluntarily or they go to court and get a judgment. As a matter of strategy, however, you are probably best off inviting them to come and pick the furniture up. Unless they think you will never work again, they will not do this. The $1,000 debt is much more valuable than $350 worth of junky furniture. Remember, we learned in Chapter 5 that if they take the furniture, the $1,000 debt is completely cancelled. Therefore, where the secured item has little cash value, your negotiations are going to be almost the same as if it did not exist.

Now let's assume that the furniture pledged as security is quite valuable and includes a color TV, a stereo in good condition, and has a resale value of close to $1,000. Now the collection agency would be more willing to take the security. Oh, they would still prefer money, because this saves them the trouble of picking up and selling the furniture, but their bargaining position is far stronger and they have little motive to settle the claim much below the $1,000 total.

3. Collection Agency Harassment— Legal and Illegal*

Collection agencies make a living by harassing people. Often there is a fine line separating harassing conduct that is legal from that which is illegal. If you can catch a collection agency on the wrong side of this line, you can often get the debt in question wiped out by being smart and aggressive.

A collection agency can contact you by mail and demand payment, or they can phone you. BUT YOU CAN STOP A COLLECTION AGENCY FROM COMMUNICATING WITH YOU ENTIRELY BY SIMPLY TELLING THEM SO IN

WRITING (see sample letter, following). After this, they can no longer contact you except to tell you that they are taking some specific action, such as filing papers in court, or garnishing your wages.

Bluebeard's Collection Agency
49 Pirate St.
Hooksville, California

Dear Sirs:

I have received numerous phone calls and several letters from you concerning several debts that I haven't paid. As I have repeatedly informed you, I am not able to pay these bills.

Accordingly, under 15 USC 1692C, this is my formal notice to you to CEASE ALL FURTHER COMMUNICATION with me except for the reasons specifically set forth in the federal law.

Very truly yours,

Lynn Smith

A debt collector cannot legally do any of the following:

a. Use obscene or profane language;

b. Threaten to harm you or any family member or friend;

c. Threaten to publish, or actually publish your name publicly as a person who does not pay bills;

d. Claim to be law enforcement officers of any kind or in any way suggest that they are connected with any federal, state, county or local government;**

e. Send you any written document

---

* No collection agency can legally contact you about a bill that you tell them you don't owe until they send you proof of the debt, such as a copy of an unpaid bill. If you are confused about whether you owe money or not, you are entitled to ask for, and receive, a full statement as to the details of the alleged debt.

** Anyone that makes this sort of claim on any debt except a debt for child support is almost surely lying. Ask for names, badge numbers, supervisor's names, etc., and check it out.

that looks like a court form or government document;

f. Repeatedly use the telephone to annoy you;

g. Contact your employer, except to verify employment or for some act (i.e., a wage garnishment) necessary to actually collect the debt;

h. Threaten to get welfare or unemployment benefits cut off (this of course can't be done);

i. Call you at work if you or your employer tell them not to. If this becomes a problem, put your request in writing and keep a copy;

j. Falsely pretend that you have committed a crime;

k. Falsely pretend that a legal action is being started against you when this is not true;*

l. Threaten to take your property [i.e., your wages unless they have a court judgment (see Chapters 8 and 9)];

m. Claim to be an attorney or use attorney's stationery when they are not;

n. Falsely claim that the debt will be increased by the addition of attorney's fees, service fees, finance charges, etc;

That collection agencies are not supposed to do any of the above doesn't mean they don't. In fact, abusive practices are still all too common. The authors of this book have seen all the above list used against low income people. It has been particularly common to send people fake legal papers or to call them and pretend to be a law enforcement officer. People are told, for example, that if they don't make a payment immediately, the sheriff will come and take all their furniture away or will have their wages immediately attached. That sort of thing is not still done, you say? Well, several Southern California collectors have been caught pretending to be peace officers and have had their licenses suspended. Vulgarity and profanity are also common, as are veiled threats against the debtor or members of his family. For example, if a collector knows that a debtor's son works for the highway patrol, he might threaten to tell the patrol that his parents are deadbeats. Tactics like this are completely illegal.

Fortunately, the State of California and the federal government have finally started to assume some responsibility to regulate the worst abuses of collection agencies. After years of doing nothing, they have begun to clean things up a little. If you believe you have been treated unfairly by a collector, contact:**

State of California Collection
and Investigative Services
1920 20th Street
Sacramento, CA 95814
(916) 739-3028

State of California Office
of the Attorney General
1515 "K" St.
Sacramento, CA 95814

and either:

Federal Trade Commission
11000 Wilshire Blvd.
Los Angeles, CA 90024

or

Federal Trade Commission
450 Golden Gate Ave.
Box 36005
San Francisco, CA 94102

---

* A bill collector was held to have violated the Fair Debt Collection Practices Act by falsely threatening legal action and failing to inform the debtor of his right to dispute the debt. BAKER V. G.E. SERVICES CORP (1982) 677 F.2d 775, 9th Cir.

** The state and federal rules are very similar, but the California rules apply to all debt collectors (collection agencies and the original creditor) while the feds only regulate collection agencies. It's always best to complain to both agencies if you have a problem. The California rules are contained in Civil Code Section 1788; the Federal law can be found at 15 U.S.C.Sec.1692.

After you make your complaint, you will be supplied a complaint form and will be given help in dealing with the obnoxious collector. If the state agencies drag their feet, contact the local office of your State Senator or Assemblyman and tell them your problem. They will make sure that a thorough investigation of your complaint is made. Remember, keep all documents that shed light on your complaint and try, if possible, to have a friend listen in on any abusive oral conversations with the collection agency.

Collectors are used to bullying people. They don't know what to do when you take the offensive. Any time you have a well-documented case of harassment, turn the tables on them. After complaining to the state and the F.T.C., try to get an attorney to represent you in a damage suit against the collection agency in either state or federal court (attorney fees and court costs can be recovered if you win). You are entitled to any actual damages (including pain and suffering) that you experience and up to $1000 in punitive damages. The creditor may be imprisoned and fined up to $2,500 if the violation was that they sent you a written document that appeared to be a court form, government document, or attorney's letter but it was not. Perhaps a more satisfying alternative would be to bring your own case to Small Claims Court. At the very least, write the original creditor and tell them what happened, sending a copy of the letter to the collection agency, the State Bureau of Collection and Investigative Services, your local State Senator and Assemblyman, and the Federal Trade Commission. If you persist and make enough of an issue out of it, you are likely to get the whole debt cancelled in exchange for shutting up. We have seen this approach work many times, as the original creditor may well be as disturbed by the collection agency's tactics as you are. A sample letter follows.

15 Main Street
Los Angeles, California
July 12, 19__

Trueshine Furniture Factory
11 Maple Street
Cedarville, California

Dear Sirs:

On May 10, 19__ I purchased a living room set from your company for $1,000 ($500 down and the rest at $50 per month.) Soon after the purchase, I lost my job and later became ill. I have had no money since to pay you. In 19__, I was contacted by the Bluebeard Bloodhound Collection Agency. They called me often, used profanity to me, my husband, and my eleven-year-old son. In addition, they sent a man to my house who claimed to be a county employee to get the furniture and on several occasions have called my father and threatened him with a law suit, even though he is a 76-year-old diabetic with a heart condition and has had no connection with this transaction.

I have contacted the State of California Bureau of Collections and Investigative Services and they are conducting an investigation. In the meantime, I am considering seeing an attorney. Frankly, I am at my wits end with these people and am fully prepared to take any steps necessary to protect myself and my family from further harassment. I am writing you in the hope that you have not condoned Bluebeard Bloodhound's practices and can do something to help me.

Very truly yours,

Lynn Smith

copies sent to:

_____, State Assemblyman
California Bureau of Collection and Investigative Services
Bluebeard Bloodhound Collections
Federal Trade Commission

4. Turning the Tables on the Collection Agency

Unfortunately, there is still a good deal a collection agency can do to be unpleasant without engaging in illegal activity. Phone calls and dun letters are bad enough. But remember, the collection agency is trying to get you upset. Just relax, don't let the letters get to you, and hang up the phone as soon as you realize who is calling.

Here is an example of an actual conversation a friend of ours had with a bill collector. (We will call our friend "S"; "BC" stands for Bill Collector.)

BC: Hello, Mr. "S," I am calling about your charge account. It's overdue.

S: Yes, I know.

BC: Well, when can we expect a payment?

S: Not for another month or two.

BC: I'm sorry but we cannot accept that.

S: Well, there's nothing else I can do. We just don't have any money right now and won't have any next month.

BC: What is the problem, Mr. "S"?

S: It's personal and I would rather not talk about it.

BC: You realize that your credit rating will fall because of this.

S: Yes, I know, but I have no interest in buying more things on credit.

BC: And that it will hinder you from getting credit at other places.

S: Yes, but I just don't have any money right now and I am tired of paying high interest anyway.

BC: We can also attach your wages.

S: Yes, but not until you get a judgment and that takes time.

BC: Why, we have a battery of lawyers and can send them to court in fifteen minutes.

S: Yes, but you still must first serve me with papers, have a trial, and get a judgment before you can attach. This take 30 days from the time you serve me with the papers, which you have not done yet.

BC: You think you're so smart. Why, we can call your employer.

S: Yes, but you can only do it once.

BC: How did you know that? Oh (mumble, mumble), but once is enough anyway.

S: And besides, you don't know who my employer is.

BC: Oh, we have ways of finding out.

S: And besides he wouldn't care.

Click--the bill collector hung up.

The bill collector tried to frighten the debtor with talk about his credit rating, attachment of his wages and calling his employer. But none worked. And so, having gone through his scare list with no results, the bill collector freaked out and, not knowing what else to say, hung up the phone.

A little laughter will often flip them out completely. We know of one person who simply called the collection agency three times for every time they called her and wasted as much of the agency's time as possible. She would also write poems about how uptight collection agencies are on the bottom of all the letters they sent and sent them back to the agency in an envelope with no stamp. Pretty soon every time she called, the collection agency would slam down the phone. Use your head, you're not helpless and you are only a victim if you let yourself be.

chapter 8

$ $ $ $ $ $

The Law Suit

If you fail to pay debts, you will probably be sued sooner or later. This is because the creditor, with the exception of the tax man, can't go after your wages, bank account or property until he has sued you and gotten a judgment. The period during which you can be sued ("statute of limitations") varies greatly for different sorts of debts. On written contracts (this covers almost everything you buy on credit), a law suit must be filed within four years or it is barred.* The statute of limitation period on oral contracts (i.e., an oral rental contract) is two years; on most personal injury claims, such as auto accidents, it is one year; and for property damage claims it is three years.** The various statutes of limi-

tation on student loans are discussed in Chapter 15. To figure when the statute of limitations runs out, start counting from the day the loan was due. If payments are involved, this means from the date you missed the payment.*** But be careful, you can voluntarily extend (revive) the statute of limitations if you agree to pay the debt in writing after the limitations period has run out.*** We are often asked if simply making a payment after the statute of limitations period has expired without entering into a new written agreement will reinstate the debt. The answer is "No."

EXAMPLE 1: Aaron buys furniture from Baron's on a written installment contract. Aaron pays Baron's for one year

---

* Code of Civil Procedure Section 337.

** See Code of Civil Procedure Sections 338, 339, 339.5, 340.

*** Code of Civil Procedure Section 360.

and then ceases making payments. Baron's has the right to sue Aaron for four years from the date of the missed payment. After that, the suit is barred by the statute of limitations.

EXAMPLE 2: Same example, but after Aaron hasn't paid Baron's for five years, Baron's writes Aaron a note and asks for a small payment as a token of good faith. Aaron sends $10. Can Baron's now sue Aaron? No, simply making a payment doesn't revive the right to sue, but if Aaron sent a note back to Baron's with the money, saying that he would pay so much each month, the right to sue would be revived.

EXAMPLE 3: Same example, but Aaron hasn't paid Baron's for three years. Baron's calls and asks for money and says that in exchange for a monthly payment and a waiver of the statute of limitations for four years, he will hold off on suing Aaron and attaching his wages. Aaron agrees and signs a paper extending the statute of limitations. Is this waiver binding? Yes. Section 360.5 of the Code of Civil Procedure allows for written waivers of the statute of limitations to be made for up to four years. Written waivers may be made either before or after the statute of limitations expires and may be renewed for an additional period of not to exceed four years.

The law suit starts when a creditor or his lawyer fills in a complaint form, takes it to the Court Clerk, pays a filing fee, and has a copy of the papers served to you, along with another document known as a "Summons." All complaint forms involving non-payment of debts are similar. Only the name of the creditor and the defendant (that's you), the dates, subject of dispute, and amounts owed change. The following paragraphs discuss this process in a little more detail.

A. Receiving the Complaint

The defendant (debtor) must be served with papers telling him what the plaintiff (creditor) is upset about. In Small Claims Court, this is done either by handing the papers to the defendant, or by sending them to him via certified mail. In Municipal or Superior Court the rules of service are a little stricter. Here the defendant must be handed the papers personally, or, if he can't be located, the papers may be handed to a person at least 18 years of age at the defendant's home or business and another copy mailed to the defendant.

In many cases, the plaintiff will first mail a copy of the summons and complaint to the defendant with an accompanying form called an "Acknowledgement of Service of Summons." This procedure, authorized by Code of Civil Procedure Section 415.30, is intended to save the expense of having the summons and complaint personally served on the defendant. If the defendant signs the papers, then he or she is deemed "served" on the date of signature. If the defendant refuses to sign and the plaintiff can later establish that the papers were received, the defendant will be responsible for the costs of personal service. Since these usually run from between $25 and $100, it is often a good idea to sign the Acknowledgement and send it to the address indicated.

If you want to better understand the technicalities of service, go to a law library and check California Code of Civil Procedure Sections 413.10-417.40. Once issued by a court, papers must be served on you within three years to be valid (C.C.P 581a). Once served, the plaintiff has an additional three years in which to get a judgment if you fail to respond. If he doesn't, the case shall be dismissed (C.C.P. 581a).

B. Which Court Are You Being Sued in?

Where you are sued depends primarily on the amount of money in dispute:

1. SMALL CLAIMS COURT: Disputes involving $1,500 or less, or where a creditor with a claim larger than $1,500 decides to permanently give up his claim to all amounts over $1,500. No one is required to use Small Claims Court. A $200 case, for example, could be started in either Small Claims or Municipal Court.

2. JUSTICE COURT: Exists only in rural areas, where Municipal Courts and Small Claims Courts have not been set up. Creditors can sue for $25,000 or less.

3. MUNICIPAL COURT: Disputes involving $25,000 or less.

4. SUPERIOR COURT: Disputes involving $25,000 or more.

C. What Papers Are You Served with?

In Small Claims Court, you will be served with a document called the "Plaintiff's Statement." In Municipal and Superior Court, you will receive at least two documents. The top document is one page and is called a "Summons."

It tells you how long you have to respond to the complaint (30 days except in landlord-tenant unlawful detainer cases), and to whom your response should be addressed. The document underneath the summons (usually several pages) is called a complaint, and contains a number of statements (called allegations) supporting the plaintiff's request for judgment against you. Additionally, if the suit has been brought in Municipal Court, you may also receive two forms called "Case Questionnaires". One of these will be filled out by the plaintiff, and one will be blank. If the plaintiff has filled his or hers out, you will be required to fill in the blank one and send it back to the plaintiff (or the plaintiff's attorney). We will tell you how to do this a little later in this chapter.

D. Reading the Complaint

In Small Claims Court, complaints are easy to read. The amount in dispute and the reason for the debts are both clearly stated. Complaints filed in Municipal or Superior Court are often harder to figure out, as they are full of legal jargon. Don't be intimidated, most of the words are not important. Sometimes complaints are divided into sections called "Causes of Action." This normally means that you are being sued for more than one thing in the same complaint. All you really need to know is:

1. Who is suing you;

2. The reason for the suit;

3. How much you are being sued for;

4. The court you are being sued in.

On the first page, you will be told the name of the Court and the name of the person suing. This person is called the "Plaintiff" and his or her name appears at the top of the box on the first page.

NOTE: The following is the top half of the first page of the form complaint being used more and more frequently by attorneys. In some cases, attorneys will use their own format for this part of the complaint, but the information you'll be interested in will be located in essentially the same place.

ATTORNEY OR PARTY WITHOUT ATTORNEY (NAME AND ADDRESS)	TELEPHONE	FOR COURT USE ONLY
ATTORNEY FOR (NAME)		
Insert name of court, judicial district or branch court, if any, and post office and street address:		
PLAINTIFF		
DEFENDANT		
☐ DOES 1 TO _____		
CONTRACT ☐COMPLAINT ☐CROSS-COMPLAINT	CASE NUMBER	

Sometimes the person suing (the plaintiff) will not be a name you recognize. This may be because the original creditor has sold the account to the plaintiff. This is legal, but if it has been done, it must be so stated in one of the first few numbered paragraphs.

Read through all the paragraphs to find out what the plaintiff claims the money is owed for. This usually appears in the middle and is often surrounded by a bunch of legal jargon, but if you slow down and read carefully, you will figure it out. To find out the total amount owed, look at the last page of the complaint for the word "WHEREFORE," in capital letters. Here it states the total amount that the creditor claims you owe. See the hypothetical complaint in Section G below.

E. If You Feel You Owe the Money

In a great many cases where a debtor is sued, the money is properly owed. In this situation, you can proceed in one or more of the following ways:

1. Do Nothing

If you fail to respond to the complaint, you will automatically lose the case and a judgment will be taken against you for the amount set out in the complaint, plus court costs and attorney fees if there was a credit agreement calling for them. Once the creditor gets the judgment he can go after your bank account, wages, or property (see Chapters 10 and 11).

While in the short run this may be little to worry about if you are judgment proof (see Chapter 1), remember that judgments are good for ten years, are renewable, and can therefore cause you trouble down the line if you should come into some money. If you are planning on filing for bankruptcy (see Chapter 18), however, the judgment will be cancelled (discharged) unless it involves taxes, family support obligations, or student loans [see Chapter 18 for a further discussion of bankruptcy].

2. Try to Settle with the Creditor

In Chapter 7, we discuss this procedure. If you offer to pay cash, the creditor will normally accept considerably less than the total and/or be willing to let you pay the debt off over time. In such an event, however, the creditor will usually insist that you agree or "stipulate" to the judgment being obtained and filed so that if you fail to meet your obligations, he or she will at least have a judgment to enforce.

3. Have an Attorney Negotiate for You

By threatening bankruptcy, indicating that he or she may oppose the suit, or just generally knowing how to throw sand in the air, an attorney may well be able to make a settlement for far less than the total debt. This approach depends on your having enough money to make a lump sum settlement offer, or at least enough to make substantial payments (see Chapter 13).

F. If You Feel You Have a Defense

1. Small Claims Court

If you are sued in Small Claims Court, you need file no written response. Just show up on the day of the hearing and tell your story to the judge. This is the time to bring letters, photographs, and witnesses. No lawyers are allowed either side and the proceedings are fairly informal. See Chapter 2, Section B, and get a copy of EVERYBODY'S GUIDE TO SMALL CLAIMS COURT (see back of this book). If you lose, you may request that the judge allow you to pay off the debt with small monthly payments.

Also, if you feel you should have won, you may appeal to the Superior Court for a brand new trial. Under California Court Rule 155, the Superior Court proceedings are supposed to be conducted informally, the same as in the Small Claims Court, but each side can be represented by an attorney and is entitled to a jury trial. Again, see EVERYBODY'S GUIDE TO SMALL CLAIMS COURT.

2. Municipal or Superior Court

If you are sued in Municipal or Superior Court, you must file a <u>written</u> answer in the correct form within 30 days from the time the papers are served on you. The creditor will win the case by default if no written answer is filed within the 30 days, unless you file papers to set aside the judgment right away and give the court a valid reason, such as illness, for failing to respond within the first thirty days.* Normally you will need an attorney to do this. You had your chance to tell your story to the judge, and you blew it.

You can, of course, represent yourself in Municipal or Superior Court if you can't, or don't want to pay a lawyer and are not eligible for legal aid. To do this, you would file your own answer and then appear in court by yourself. We know many people who have successfully advocated their own cases and we are very supportive of the idea that courts should welcome everyone. But we want to remind you that courts can be difficult for non-lawyers to deal with. It is a sad commentary on our laws and civilization that it is so difficult for ordinary folk to speak for themselves, especially when you consider that it need not be this way.

If you want to go ahead and represent yourself, more power to you. Many others have managed it successfully. In this book, we will only discuss a few fundamental procedures necessary for you to get into and remain in court. There may be a number of other possibilities in your particular case, but they are beyond the scope of these materials. If you desire to defend your case in a more sophisticated manner, including the making of legal motions and the raising of affirmative defenses, go to a law library and ask to see the Continuing Education of the Bar (C.E.B.) volumes on CIVIL PRACTICE BEFORE TRIAL and CIVIL TRIALS. Other resources are also available, such as WITKIN ON CALIFORNIA PROCEDURES, and CALIFORNIA FORMS OF PLEADING AND PRACTICE. These books contain information and authorities on various

concepts of law and possible defenses, with copies of the relevant law and useful forms. Look in the index under the subjects that interest you. You will find LEGAL RESEARCH: HOW TO FIND AND UNDERSTAND THE LAW by Elias, Nolo Press (see back of this book) helpful in using the law library and deciphering the law. If you have trouble, ask the law librarian for help.

MUNICIPAL COURT NOTE: A set of simple procedures which make it possible to represent yourself apply to all cases filed in Municipal Court. See Section H below for more on these.

Regardless of which court you are sued in, your answer must be filed within 30 days after you are served with court papers (if the 30th day falls on a weekend or holiday, you may file on the next business day).

Your answer must be filed within 30 days after you are served with court papers (if the 30th day falls on a weekend or holiday, you may file on the next business day).

Specific forms have been prepared for your use. Because almost all actions by a creditor will be based on a contract which you allegedly breached, you will want to use the form entitled "ANSWER-- Contract." Where do you get this form? We have included one in the Appendix for your convenience. Also, it can be obtained from your closest Municipal or Superior Court.

The ANSWER--Contract form is also reproduced on the following pages. As you can see, it consists of two pages (front and back). At the top of the first page you should put your name, address, telephone number, and the Latin phrase "in pro per" after "Attorney For (Name)".* Then follow these steps carefully:

---

* Code of Civil Procedure Section 473 sets out the actual grounds for setting aside a judgment.

* In pro per is short for "in propria persona," which literally means "in one's own proper person," and effectivly means "by yourself."

Page two

SHORT TITLE: | CASE NUMBER

ANSWER—Contract

4. ☐ AFFIRMATIVE DEFENSES
Defendant alleges the following additional reasons that plaintiff is not entitled to recover anything:

☐ Continued on Attachment 4.

5. ☐ Other:

6. DEFENDANT PRAYS
a. that plaintiff take nothing.
b. ☐ for costs of suit.
c. ☐ other (specify):

.... | ....
(Type or print name) | (Signature of party or attorney)

Page two

ATTORNEY OR PARTY WITHOUT ATTORNEY (NAME AND ADDRESS) | TELEPHONE | FOR COURT USE ONLY

ATTORNEY FOR (NAME):

Insert name of court, judicial district or branch court, if any, and post office and street address:

PLAINTIFF:

DEFENDANT:

ANSWER—Contract
☐ TO COMPLAINT OF (name):
☐ TO CROSS-COMPLAINT OF (name):

CASE NUMBER

1. This pleading, including attachments and exhibits, consists of the following number of pages:

2. DEFENDANT (name)

answers the complaint or cross-complaint as follows:

3. **Check ONLY ONE of the next two boxes:**
a. ☐ Defendant generally denies each statement of the complaint or cross-complaint *(Do not check this box if the verified complaint or cross-complaint demands more than $1,000.)*
b. ☐ Defendant admits that all of the statements of the complaint or cross-complaint are true EXCEPT
(1) Defendant claims the following statements are false *(use paragraph numbers or explain)*:

☐ Continued on Attachment 3 b (1)

(2) Defendant has no information or belief that the following statements are true, so defendant denies them *(use paragraph numbers or explain)*.

☐ Continued on Attachment 3 b (2)
(Continued)

If this form is used to answer a cross-complaint, plaintiff means cross-complainant and defendant means cross-defendant
Form Approved by the
Judicial Council of California
Effective January 1, 1982
Rule 982.1(35)

ANSWER—Contract

CCP 425.12

STEP 1: In the part of the Answer where it says to insert the name of the court, etc., put the name and address of the court where the action has been brought. Copy this from the first page of the Complaint served on you. It will say something like, "Municipal Court of the State of California, County of San Mateo, Northern Judicial District".

STEP 2: In the part of the Answer labelled "Plaintiff," put the exact name of the plaintiff as it appears on the first page of the Complaint. It will say something like, "Joe Schmerd, Plaintiff v. John Smith, Defendant".

STEP 3: In the part of the Answer labelled "Defendant," put your name as it appears on the complaint. If your name is misspelled, you will be able to correct this at a later time. The fact that your name may be misspelled does not affect the validity of the complaint, however.

STEP 4: In the part of the Answer labelled "Case Number," put the number which appears on the Complaint or on the summons attached to the front of the Complaint.

STEP 5: Check the box in front of "TO COMPLAINT OF (NAME):" and put the plaintiff's name in after the colon.

STEP 6: Item #1 of the Answer asks for the number of pages which you are submitting as part of your Answer. Since you won't know this for sure until you have completed the Answer, leave it blank for now, but don't forget to come back and fill it in later. Usually, you will only be submitting the two pages (usually front and back).

STEP 7: Put your name in the space provided in item #2 of the Answer.

STEP 8: Item #3 of the Answer asks you to respond to the specific statements contained in the Complaint. We recommend that you check box "b" and then carefully read the Complaint and separate the paragraphs into four groups.

■ The first group should include the paragraphs which contain statements known by you to be true. Usually, these will include the paragraphs about your identity, your address, and the fact that you signed an agreement of some type.

■ The second group should include every paragraph containing statements with which you disagree. These typically will be the paragraphs about the agreement being valid and legal, about your owing a particular sum of money, and about your having received what you paid for.

■ The third group will be those paragraphs which contain some statements with which you agree and others with which you disagree. For example, if the statement is made that you signed a valid agreement, you may agree that you signed an agreement, but disagree about its validity.

■ The fourth group will be those statements which you really know nothing about, such as actions taken by the creditor without your knowledge.

STEP 9: Once you have analyzed the complaint as we suggest here, do the following:

■ Place the number of each paragraph contained in your second group (the ones you disagree with) in the space provided under 3(b)(1) of the Answer.

■ In the space that's left in 3(b)(1), take the third group and identify them with the following language: "I also deny paragraph "X" except that __[put in reason]__. "I also deny paragraph "Y" except that __[put in reason]__. If you need more room, take a clean, white 8 ½" x 11" piece of paper, label it "Attachment 3(b)(1)" and continue until you're through with the third group.

Take the fourth group of paragraphs and list their numbers in the space provided under 3(b)(2) in the Answer. If you need more room, make an attachment as suggested above and label it "Attachment 3(b)(2)."

NOTE: You can put several "attachments" on one piece of paper so long as they're clearly labeled.

Now, go to the second page of the Answer (usually on the back of the first page). At the top, put the plaintiff's name, vs., and your name (e.g., Jones vs. Smith) and the case number, and then proceed to the next step.

STEP 10: In item #4 of the Answer you are required to list any "affirmative defenses" you might wish to raise. What is an affirmative defense? Any reason why the plaintiff shouldn't recover all or part of what the complaint asks for is an affirmative defense unless it can fairly be implied from your denials in item #3 of the Answer. To be on the safe side, briefly summarize all your positions here, so the court and the creditor will know why you're contesting the action.

The following are examples of affirmative defenses which you might have in your case:

1. You never received the goods or services that the creditor claims he provided;

2. The goods or services provided you were seriously defective;

3. As part of the delivering of the goods or services, the creditor damaged your property or possessions;

4. You were charged excessive interest;

5. Serious misrepresentations were made by the creditor to get you to sign in the first place.

CO-SIGNER NOTE: Non-English speakers being sued as co-signers had a right (for all obligations co-signed after January 1, 1986) to receive notice describing their obligation at the time they co-signed. The lack of such a notice may provide them with an affirmative defense. Civil Code Sections 1799.91 through 1799.99 (effective 1/1/86).

If you need more room, make an attachment as suggested earlier.

STEP 11: Skip Number 5 and proceed to item #6. Here you are asked to specify what you want the court to do. Normally, when you are representing yourself, you will simply want to check Box b and not specify any other relief.

STEP 12: Type or print your name on the bottom lefthand line, and sign on the right. Make sure your signature is exactly the same as your typed name. Don't type John B. Smith and sign John Smith.

Now go back to the first page and put the number of pages (two or more) which you will be submitting.

STEP 13: In most Municipal Court actions (with the exception of unlawful detainer cases), you will not need to sign a verification (i.e., a statement under penalty of perjury that your answer is true). In Superior Court cases, however, you will also need to sign a verification if the Complaint is verified. If you are in Superior Court or are involved in an unlawful detainer action, type out the following statement on a separate piece of paper, sign it, and attach it to your Answer:

VERIFICATION

I am (a) defendant in the above action; I have read the foregoing Answer, and know the contents thereof; and I certify that the same is true of my own knowledge.

I certify, under penalty of perjury, that the foregoing is true and correct.

Executed on _____(date)_____, 19___, at _____(place)_____, California.

_____
Defendant

STEP 14: If you have also been served with a blank case questionnaire in addition to a summons and complaint, now is the time to fill it in. See the instructions that follow.

Under new Municipal Court rules, the plaintiff has the option of filling out a "case questionnaire" and serving it on you along with the Summons and Complaint. If this option is exercised, then you also have to fill out one of these questionnaires. If the plaintiff doesn't fill out a case questionnaire, you don't either. For once, a legal form has been designed which is basically self explanatory. Almost all the questions can be answered without too much fuss. Accordingly, we will only

---

— DO NOT FILE WITH THE COURT —

PLAINTIFF:	CASE NUMBER
DEFENDANT:	

— QUESTIONS —

1. FOR ALL CASES
a. State your name and street address.

b. State your current business name and street address, type of business entity, and your title.

c. Describe in detail your claims or defenses and the facts on which they are based, giving relevant dates.
☐ See attachment for answer number 1c.

d. State the name, street address, and telephone number of each person who has knowledge of facts relating to this lawsuit and specify his or her area of knowledge.
☐ See attachment for answer number 1d.

e. Describe each document or photograph that relates to the issues or facts. You are encouraged to attach a copy of each. For each that you have described but not attached, state the name, street address, and telephone number of each person who has it.
☐ See attachment for answer number 1e.

982(a)(2) (New July 1. 1983)   **CASE QUESTIONNAIRE**   Page two of four

1. f. Describe each item of physical evidence that relates to the issues and facts, give its location, and state the name, street address, and telephone number of each person who has it.

☐ See attachment for answer number 1f.

g. State the name and street address of each insurance company and the number of each policy that may cover you in whole or part for the damages claimed.

☐ See attachment for answer number 1g.

2. FOR PERSONAL INJURY OR PROPERTY DAMAGE CASES

a. Describe each injury or illness that you received and your present complaints about each.

☐ See attachment for answer number 2a.

b. State the name, street address, and telephone number of each physician, dentist, or other health care provider who treated or examined you, the type of treatment, the dates of treatment, and the charges by each to date.

☐ See attachment for answer number 2b.

c. Itemize the medical expenses you anticipate in the future.

☐ See attachment for answer number 2c.

d. Itemize your loss of income to date, give the name and street address of each source, and show how the loss is computed.

☐ See attachment for answer number 2d.

982(a)(21) (New July 1, 1983)

CASE QUESTIONNAIRE

---

2. e. Itemize the loss of income you anticipate in the future, give the name and street address of each source, and show how the loss is computed.

☐ See attachment for answer number 2e.

f. Itemize your property damage and state the amount or attach an itemized bill or estimate.

☐ See attachment for answer number 2f.

g. Describe each other item of damage or cost that you claim and state the amount.

☐ See attachment for answer number 2g.

3. FOR CASES BASED ON AGREEMENTS

a. In addition to your answer to 1e, state all the terms and give the date of any part of the agreement that is not in writing.

☐ See attachment for answer number 3a.

b. Describe each item of damage or cost you claim, state the amount, and show how it is computed.

☐ See attachment for answer number 3b.

VERIFICATION

I declare under penalty of perjury under the laws of the State of California that the foregoing answers are true and correct.

Date:

....

(TYPED OR PRINTED NAME)

▲

_____
(SIGNATURE)

982(a)(21) (New July 1, 1983)

CASE QUESTIONNAIRE

comment on questions which we think might require a little guidance.

A CAUTIONARY NOTE: When you fill out and sign this form, you are doing so under penalty of perjury. You will be bound by your statements in the lawsuit and will be able to change them only with great difficulty. For this reason, we strongly suggest you take your time and make sure you are giving correct information. You needn't volunteer information which isn't asked for in the questions. In order to determine how detailed your information should get, study the plaintiff's questionnaire (remember, if the plaintiff didn't fill one out, then you don't need to either). If the information is very cursory and not detailed, then yours needn't be either. Good luck.

Question 1C: In this question you are asked to describe your claims or defenses in detail and the facts on which they are based, giving relevant dates. If your "ANSWER" simply consisted of denials, then here is where you should explain why (i.e., I paid the bill already, etc.). If, on the other hand, you incorporated "affirmative defenses" in your Answer, then you may have already provided the detail requested here, and unless you have anything to add, such as dates, times, or specific names of persons, you can simply refer to the specific affirmative defense contained in the Answer.

Question 1D: This question does not require you to run out and do research in order to get the information requested, but you should provide it if you're able. The same goes for the other questions asking for specific information. Make a good faith effort to provide the information, but you're not expected to locate information not reasonably available.

Question 2: This question and its subparts are concerned with cases involving personal injury and property damage claims. In most cases, your claim will arise from a breach of contract or agreement and you will thus probably want to skip these questions and go right to Question 3 and its subparts.

Question 3A: In many cases, your defense will involve oral representations by a salesman which were not put into the written agreement signed by you. Here is your chance to specify any such representation and exactly how you relied on it in making your deal.

Question 3B: If you are claiming that you were damaged in some way by the transaction which led to the lawsuit, here is your chance to specify that damage. However, if you have been damaged, you probably should have filed a cross-complaint against the plaintiff. If you have not, then you will not be allowed to recover any damages you suffered.

STEP 15: Before the Court will allow you to file your Answer, it will need to know that you have caused a copy of it to be delivered to the plaintiff or the plaintiff's lawyer. This is usually done by mail, and must be done by someone who is not a party (i.e., actually named as a defendant) in the case.

To satisfy this requirement, type out the following statement on a separate piece of paper, fill in the blanks as shown below, and attach it to your answer:

PROOF OF SERVICE BY MAIL

I am a citizen of the United States and a resident of the county of _____ _____. I am over the age of 18 years and not a party to the above action; my residence address is: _____ _____, California. On _____, 198_, I served the within Answer on the Plaintiffs in said action by placing a true copy thereof enclosed in a sealed envelope with postage thereon fully prepaid, in the United States post office mail box at ___[city]___, California, addressed as follows:

①

_____
I, ___[name of sender]___, certify under penalty of perjury that the foregoing is true and correct. Executed on __[date]__, 198_, at ____[city]____, California.

②

_____
[signature]

1. Enter here the name of the creditor or his attorney as it appears in the upper left of the first page of the Complaint.

2. Signature of person mailing Answer to plaintiffs.

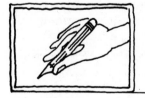

CHECK LIST:

You should have the following documents:

■ At least two pages of Answer (more if there are attachments);

■ A verification if the case is in Superior Court or involves an unlawful detainer action and the Complaint is verified;

■ A Case Questionnaire if one has been sent to you and the plaintiff has also filled one out;

■ A Proof of Service.

Make at least two photocopies of the entire packet of papers to be served on the plaintiff. One set should be mailed to the plaintiff or his/her attorney (whose address will appear at the top of the Complaint and on the Summons) by the person signing the Proof of Service.

STEP 16: Once you have served your Answer on the plaintiff or plaintiff's attorney (in most cases), you'll need to file your Answer with the court. This will involve paying a fee which is fairly sizable in Superior Court. Before you go to the court, call and find out what it will cost. Then take your original Answer and at least one copy, along with a check, money order, or cash, to the clerk for the appropriate court.

When you get to the right clerk's office, give them the Original and one copy. The clerk will examine the original to make sure a "Proof of Service" is attached and should then stamp it "Filed" in the empty box in the top righthand corner. In most cases, the clerk will tell you to "file stamp" your copy yourself; at other times they will do it for you. This file-stamped copy is your proof that you filed an answer.

POVERTY NOTE: All courts have a way for poor people to get their day in court without paying filing fees if they are unable to. To do so, you will need to proceed "in forma pauperis". This means that you'll have to fill out an application and a statement under oath detailing your income and expenses so that the court can ascertain your inability to afford the filing fee. The

clerk should have the necessary forms
for you to get the filing fees waived
under this procedure. Just ask.

G. Hypothetical Case

1. The Facts

Suppose you, Constance Computerphobe,
decide to give yourself a computer for
a Christmas present. In early December
1984, after weeks of agonizing computer
shopping, you are sold a SuperDuperMemo-
ry 50 portable for $1,500 by an engaging
salesman working at SuperComputer, a
local computer store. The salesman
assures you the machine will accept all
software written for the Apple II.

You sign a written agreement under
which you will make a down payment of
$250 and agree to pay the $1,250 balance
in equal installments of $250 over the
next five months, starting January 1,
1985. The agreement provides for no
interest, but does contain a clause
permitting SuperComputer to "accelerate"
the entire debt if you miss one payment.
After the paperwork is done and your
down payment made, you walk out with the
computer under your arm.

After wrestling with your new toy for
several days, you quickly discover it
won't run programs written for Apple
Computers. You take it back to the
store, only to learn your salesman has
left for greener pastures. The store
doesn't believe your story about what
the salesman told you and refuses to
cancel the agreement and give you your
down payment back.

You, accordingly, refuse to pay your
first installment and instead send a
short, nasty letter informing SuperComputer you will not pay anything and
demanding your down payment back in
exchange for your return of the computer. A few weeks later, you are served
with a complaint that looks like this:

2. The Complaint

ATTORNEY OR PARTY WITHOUT ATTORNEY (NAME AND ADDRESS) | TELEPHONE | FOR COURT USE ONLY

Evan Silvertongue
233 Lawyer's Row   (415) 544-7277
San Francisco, CA 94111

ATTORNEY FOR (NAME): Plaintiff: Supercomputer, Inc.

Insert name of court, judicial district or branch court, if any, and post office and street address:

Municipal Court, City and County of
San Francisco
City Hall
San Francisco, CA

PLAINTIFF

Supercomputer, Inc.

DEFENDANT

Constance Computerphobe

DOES 1 TO _____

CASE NUMBER
C 11122331

CONTRACT
[X] COMPLAINT   [ ] CROSS-COMPLAINT

1. This pleading, including attachments and exhibits, consists of the following number of pages: 3

2. a. Each plaintiff named above is a competent adult
   [ ] Except plaintiff (name):
   [ ] a corporation qualified to do business in California
   [ ] an unincorporated entity (describe):
   [ ] other (specify):

   b. [X] Plaintiff (name): Supercomputer, Inc.
   [X] has complied with the fictitious business name laws and is doing business under the fictitious name of (specify):
   [ ] has complied with all licensing requirements as a licensed (specify):

   c. [ ] Information about additional plaintiffs who are not competent adults is shown in Complaint—Attachment 2c.

3. a. Each defendant named above is a natural person
   [ ] Except defendant (name):   [ ] Except defendant (name):
   [ ] a business organization, form unknown   [ ] a business organization, form unknown
   [ ] a corporation   [ ] a corporation
   [ ] an unincorporated entity (describe):   [ ] an unincorporated entity (describe):
   [ ] a public entity (describe):   [ ] a public entity (describe):
   [ ] other (specify):   [ ] other (specify):

   b. The true names and capacities of defendants sued as Does are unknown to plaintiff.
   c. [ ] Information about additional defendants who are not natural persons is contained in Complaint—Attachment 3c.
   d. [ ] Defendants who are joined pursuant to Code of Civil Procedure section 382 are (names):

(Continued)

If this form is used as a cross-complaint, plaintiff means cross-complainant and defendant means cross-defendant.
Form Approved by the
Judicial Council of California
Effective January 1, 1982
Rule 982.1(20)

COMPLAINT—Contract

CCP 425.12

SHORT TITLE:
Supercomputer, Inc. v. Computerphobe

CASE NUMBER
11122331

COMPLAINT—Contract

Page two

4. [ ] Plaintiff is required to comply with a claims statute, and
   a. [ ] plaintiff has complied with applicable claims statutes, or
   b. [ ] [ ] plaintiff is excused from complying because (specify):

5. [ ] This action is subject to [ ] Civil Code section 1812.10 [ ] Civil Code section 2984.4.

6. [ ] This action is filed in this [X] county [ ] judicial district because
   a. [X] a defendant entered into the contract here.
   b. [ ] a defendant lived here when the contract was entered into.
   c. [ ] a defendant lives here now.
   d. [ ] the contract was to be performed here.
   e. [ ] a defendant is a corporation or unincorporated association and its principal place of business is here.
   f. [ ] real property that is the subject of this action is located here.
   g. [ ] other (specify):

7. [ ] The following paragraphs of this pleading are alleged on information and belief (specify paragraph numbers):

8. [ ] Other:

9. The following causes of action are attached and the statements above apply to each. (Each complaint must have one or more causes of action attached.)
   [X] Breach of Contract   [ ] Common Counts
   [ ] Other (specify):

10. PLAINTIFF PRAYS
    For judgment for costs of suit; for such relief as is fair, just, and equitable; and for
    [X] damages of $ 750
    [X] interest on the damages [X] according to proof [ ] at the rate of _____ percent per year
        from (date):
    [ ] attorney fees [ ] of $ _____ [ ] according to proof
    [ ] other (specify):

Evan Silvertongue
(Type or print name)

Evan Silvertongue
(Signature of plaintiff or attorney)

(If you wish to verify this pleading, affix a verification.)

Page two

3. The Answer

Your Answer should look like this:

Form 1 (Answer—Contract):

ATTORNEY OR PARTY WITHOUT ATTORNEY (NAME AND ADDRESS) | TELEPHONE | FOR COURT USE ONLY

Constance Computerphobe
237 Joost Ave.
San Francisco, CA 94117

(415) 274-0896

ATTORNEY FOR (NAME): In pro per

Insert name of court, judicial district or branch court, if any, and post office and street address:

Municipal Court, City and County of
San Francisco
City Hall
San Francisco, CA

PLAINTIFF:
Supercomputer, Inc.

DEFENDANT:
Constance Computerphobe

ANSWER—Contract

CASE NUMBER
C 1112331

[X] TO COMPLAINT OF (name): Supercomputer, Inc.
[ ] TO CROSS-COMPLAINT OF (name):

1. This pleading, including attachments and exhibits, consists of the following number of pages: 2
2. DEFENDANT (name): Constance Computerphobe

   answers the complaint or cross-complaint as follows:
3. **Check ONLY ONE of the next two boxes:**
   a. [ ] Defendant generally denies each statement of the complaint or cross-complaint. *(Do not check this box if the verified complaint or cross-complaint demands more than $1,000.)*
   b. [X] Defendant admits that all of the statements of the complaint or cross-complaint are true EXCEPT:
      (1) Defendant claims the following statements are false *(use paragraph numbers or explain)*:

      BC-2, BC-3, BC-4, and BC-6

      [ ] Continued on Attachment 3.b (1)
      (2) Defendant has no information or belief that the following statements are true, so defendant denies them *(use paragraph numbers or explain)*:

      2a, 2b, 6a

      [ ] Continued on Attachment 3.b (2).
      (Continued)

If this form is used to answer a cross-complaint, plaintiff means cross-complainant and defendant means cross-defendant.

Form Approved by the
Judicial Council of California
Effective January 1, 1982
Rule 982.1(35)

ANSWER—Contract

CCP 425.12

Form 2 (Cause of Action—Breach of Contract):

SHORT TITLE: Supercomputer, Inc. v. Computerphobe

CASE NUMBER
C 1112331

Page 3

(number)

CAUSE OF ACTION—Breach of Contract

ATTACHMENT TO [ ] Complaint [ ] Cross-Complaint

(Use a separate cause of action form for each cause of action.)

BC-1. Plaintiff *(name)*:

alleges that on or about *(date)*: December 10, 19___
a. [X] written [ ] oral [ ] other *(specify)*:
agreement was made between *(name parties to agreement)*: Supercomputer, Inc. and
Constance Computerphobe
[ ] A copy of the agreement is attached as Exhibit A, or
[X] The essential terms of the agreement [ ] are stated in Attachment BC-1 [X] are as follows *(specify)*:
1. Constance Computerphobe (Defendant) purchased one SuperDuperCompter50, serial number GT04789, from Supercomputer, Inc. for $1,500.00.
2. Pursuant to written agreement, said Defendant made a $250.00 downpayment and agreed to pay the remaining balance of $1,250.00 in five equal monthly installments of $250.00, commencing January 1, 1984.
3. Said written agreement contained an acceleration clause.

BC-2. On or about *(dates)*: January 1, 19___
defendant breached the agreement by [ ] the acts specified in Attachment BC-2 [X] the following acts *(specify)*:

Defendant refused and failed to pay the first due installment under the contract and indicated in writing she would continue to refuse to honor the terms of the agreement described above.

BC-3. Plaintiff has performed all obligations to defendant except those obligations plaintiff was prevented or excused from performing.

BC-4. Plaintiff suffered damages legally (proximately) caused by defendant's breach of the agreement
[ ] as stated in Attachment BC-4 [X] as follows *(specify)*:
$1250.00 balance due on the above described computer.

BC-5. [ ] Plaintiff is entitled to attorney fees by an agreement or a statute
[ ] of $
[ ] according to proof.

BC-6. [X] Other:
Costs according to proof.

Form Approved by the
Judicial Council of California
Effective January 1, 1982
Rule 982.1(21)

CAUSE OF ACTION—Breach of Contract

CCP 425.12

ANSWER—Contract   Page two

4. [X] AFFIRMATIVE DEFENSES
Defendant alleges the following additional reasons that plaintiff is not entitled to recover anything:

I bought the computer because the salesman said it would take Apple
software. It does not take Apple software and since the main reason I
bought the computer turned out not to be true, I should be able to return
it and get my money back.

Also, even if I am held responsible for the whole bill, the store never
sent me any notice about "accelerating" my debt, and the most I owed
them when they filed this case was $250.00.

[ ] Continued on Attachment 4.

5. [ ] Other:

6. DEFENDANT PRAYS
   a. that plaintiff take nothing.
   b. [X] for costs of suit.
   c. [ ] other (specify):

Constance Computerphobe
(Type or print name)

Constance Computerphobe
(Signature of party or attorney)

Page two

H. How to Handle Common Court Proceedings

Now that you have served and filed your answer, you will receive notification of all further proceedings in your case. In the following several paragraphs we briefly describe the most common of these proceedings and what will be expected of you. Unfortunately, a detailed account of how to cope with court procedures is beyond the scope of this book, and if your case gets complicated or confusing at some point, you'll either have to research the question yourself, using the resources mentioned earlier in this chapter, or consult a lawyer.

1. Simplified Municipal Court Procedures

All actions filed in Municipal Court (except unlawful detainer and small claims actions) are initially subject to the simplified procedures found in Code of Civil Procedure Section 90-99. Although the court may grant the plaintiff permission to prosecute the action under the formal (more complicated) rules, this permission will not normally be granted. In addition to the optional case questionnaire discussed earlier, these simplified rules provide for the following:

• sensible limitations on discovery (CCP 94. Also, see the discussion directly below);

• a fill-in-the-blanks form request (available from the clerk) which is sent to the other party and which requests a listing of the witnesses and a description of the evidence that the other party intends to present at trial (CCP 96); and

• the ability to submit certain types of testimony in writing (CCP 98).

All together, these simplified procedures make it much more feasible for a peron to represent themself than would otherwise be the case. For further information, consult BENDER'S CALIFORNIA FORMS OF PLEADING & PRACTICE, under *Municipal Courts (Economical Litigation)*.

2. General Court Procedures

In both Superior and Municipal Court, the following procedures and events typically occur in the course of the average lawsuit.

a. Discovery

Each party to a case has the right to obtain information from the other which will help in preparing for trial or settlement. This procedure, aptly called "discovery," includes depositions (requiring a person to attend a meeting and answer questions under oath), interrogatories (written questions which must be answered under oath), requests for the production of documents, requests that the other side admit or deny certain facts, and several other devices which are more rarely used, such as physical inspections of property and medical examinations.

If you fail or refuse to play the discovery game, the other side may arrange for a court hearing in which the judge will be asked to order you to comply. If you don't, then your case can be lost right there. Therefore, if the other side in your case initiates some kind of discovery, you should do your best to cope with it. The best resource in the law library to assist you with this task is the CEB publication called "Modern California Discovery." The specific statutes covering discovery are found in the Code of Civil Procedure, starting with Section 2016. Also, as we mentioned, discovery under the Simplified Municipal Court Procedures is governed by C.C.P. 94.

b. Summary Judgment

If a party is able to convince a judge there is no argument over the facts of the case (e.g., that you signed a legal contract and have failed to make the payments as provided) and that the law requires a judgment in their favor, you can lose without actually having a trial. This would happen when the other party serves you with a written paper called a "Notice of Motion and Motion for Summary Judgment" with an attached "Declaration" (statement under oath) establishing the facts necessary for the judge to rule in their favor.

When you receive these papers, you have an opportunity to file your own "Declaration" contesting the facts asserted by the other party. If you do not do this, the judge will probably rule for the other side. While this Summary Judgment can occur in the course of a court hearing at the time and place specified in the Notice of Motion and Motion for Summary Judgment, your statements in court will do you no good in the absence of a written Declaration establishing your facts.

Thus, if you are served with a Notice of Motion and Motion for Summary Judgment, make sure you respond to it in a timely and proper manner if you want to stay in court.

c. Memorandum to Set for Trial and At Issue Memorandum

Cases can't proceed to trial until a party submits a document to the court clerk telling him or her that the case can be put on the trial list. Thus, at some point in the case, you can expect to receive a document called a "Memorandum to Set for Trial" (in Municipal Court) or an "At Issue Memorandum" (in Superior Court). On this one, you don't have to do anything to stay in court, but if you disagree with any of the statements in it, such as that a jury trial is required, or that it will take two hours to try the action, you need to submit your own memorandum within 10 days.

d. Pre-Trial Settlement

Assuming you make it past the preliminary hurdles mentioned above, you will be notified of a pre-trial settlement conference sometime later in the case. This is where you and the creditor will sit down with a judge and explore whether the case can be settled. You don't have to settle, but the judge will give you some indication of where you stand and many of them are quite persuasive. Make sure and attend this conference if you want to stay in court.

e. Trial

At trial, you will need to present your case according to certain rules which have been established for the presentation of evidence. This can be tricky and very disheartening if all your hard work goes down the drain when the judge rules that your evidence is inadmissible for one reason or another. Thus, it might be worth your while to consult a lawyer before the trial about the evidence you expect to put in and get some suggestions on how to offer it. Here we only provide the following brief suggestions:

■ Organize your case so it makes sense and tells your story.

■ Bring the original of any documents you wish to present, along with two copies (one for you and one for the other side--the original will be submitted as evidence). If you don't have the original, be prepared to explain why.

■ Be prepared to explain where each document came from and why it's relevant to your case. If you wrote or received the document, you'll need to explain the circumstances. If someone other than the creditor gave you the document, that person will need to explain how they got it. The idea here is that the court needs to make sure that the document is authentic.

■ Your witnesses should all have personal knowledge of anything they are going to testify about. The court usually does not allow secondhand statements (called hearsay).

■ Any oral or written statements which have been made by either party are admissible as evidence so long as they are contained in a document or are described by the person who heard them (in the case of oral statements).

■ You should be prepared to testify that any photographs which you want to submit accurately depict what's portrayed in them. For example, if you have photographs of shoddy work done on your home which you refused to pay for, you will need to testify that the work really appears the way it looks in the photograph.

chapter 9

$ $ $ $ $ $

When There Is a Judgment Against You

Once a creditor gets a judgment against you, the law allows her additional rights in trying to collect it. As a "judgment creditor," she can direct the sheriff or marshal in your county to go after your possessions, any money you have in the bank, and up to 25% of your earnings. (All these things make up your "assets.")* She can continue her efforts to collect until she recovers the debt plus court costs and often attorney's fees. She has 10 years to collect on her judgment and can usually get an extension for an additional 10 years.

This procedure is usually known as "Attachment," and to make it as clear as possible, we have divided our discussion into three separate chapters. The first

is on wages, usually the first asset a judgment creditor goes after. The second chapter will be on "personal" property, which includes most of the things you own, like your motor vehicle, bank account, furniture, clothes, etc. The third chapter will cover "real" property, which is just a fancy legal term for your house and land.

Just as every coin has two sides, the flip side to the attachment procedure is the law on "exempt assets." Long ago the state decided that the debtor should not have to lose everything just because he owes money. After all, he still has to eat, keep a roof over his head, and provide for the family. In recognition of this, the legislature has made many assets "exempt" from attachment. Some people who don't have a lot of possessions to start with may find that most things they own are exempt.

---

* Up to 50% for child and spousal support debts.

The following three chapters will discuss which assets of yours are exempt. But one thing you should know now is that in order to take advantage of the law, you must in most instances file a "Claim of Exemption." If a judgment creditor attaches an asset of yours which under the law would be exempt and you do not file a "Claim of Exemption" in time, you lose the asset--Poof! Enough said for now. Instructions and forms for Claims of Exemption will be covered in these chapters as they become necessary.

IMPORTANT: Federal and state tax collectors can attach wages, bank accounts, personal property, and real property without getting a judgment. Claims of exemption are allowed against state tax claims but not against federal ones (see Chapter 16).

chapter 10

$ $ $ $ $ $ $

Wage Attachments

If you haven't yet done so, read Chapter 9.

Your pay check is usually the first asset a judgment creditor goes after.* It is easy to find and profitable to attach. The procedure is commonly called a "Wage Attachment," even though the correct term is "Wage Garnishment."

A. How Much Can You Lose?

Except for child support or spousal payments or taxes, no more than 25 per-

cent of your net earnings (after tax and social security deductions) can be attached (Code of Civil Procedure, Section 706.050).** If your net earnings are low, even less or nothing may be taken. The chart that follows shows you the maximum amounts that can be attached.

---

* If you work on commission, the commissions you receive are considered wages and can be attached in the same manner as wages.

** This is 50% (see Chapter 17) in the case of child and spousal support payments and state tax payments. The federal tax people can take it all if they want, but usually don't in hardship situations.

Seventy-five percent of earnings paid during the preceding 30 days or 100% of the earnings if they were subject to an earnings withholding order or wage assignment for support are also exempt under Code of Civil Procedure Section 704.070 (see Chapter 11).

ONE-WEEK PAY PERIOD

Net Earnings*	Withhold
$1.00 to $100.50	Nothing
$100.51 to $134.00	All over $100.50
$134.01 and up	25%

TWO-WEEK PAY PERIOD

Net Earnings*	Withhold
$1.00 to $201.00	Nothing
$201.01 to $268.00	All over $201.00
$268.01 and up	25%

SEMI-MONTHLY PAY PERIOD

Net Earnings*	Withhold
$1.00 to $217.75	Nothing
$217.76 to $290.33	All over $217.75
$290.34 and up	25%

MONTHLY PAY PERIOD

Net Earnings*	Withhold
$1.00 to $435.50	Nothing
$435.51 to $580.67	All over $435.50
$580.68 and up	25%

This chart is based on the federal minimum wage law which, as of January 1, 1985, is $3.35 per hour. The minimum wage may very likely rise in future years. As it does, the amounts in the chart will similarly rise. You can probably find out these new amounts by calling the sheriff or marshal's office in your county--or go to a bookstore or library, look for a later edition of this book, and just copy out the new figures.

---

* After tax and social security deductions.

B. How the Wage Attachment Procedure Works

1. A creditor has sued you on a debt and gotten a judgment against you. He or she is now a "judgment creditor."

2. Often immediately, but any time within the next ten years, assuming that the judgment creditor knows where you work, he or she can get an order from

the court to attach your wages. This is called a "Writ of Execution."

3. The creditor takes the "writ" to the sheriff or marshal, pays a fee, and instructs the sheriff or marshal to attach your wages as described in the "writ."

4. The sheriff serves your employer a copy of the "writ" and instructs him or her to withhold up to 25% of your net earnings. Your employer must send the amount withheld at each pay period to the sheriff. The sheriff will deduct expenses and give the remainder to the judgment creditor.

5. As soon as the sheriff notifies your employer of the attachment, the sheriff must also notify you.

C. Being Fired for a Wage Attachment

Often employers consider wage attachments to be a big hassle and just too much paperwork (now that most checks are made out by computer) to deduct the 25% of your net earnings each pay period and send it to the sheriff. Therefore, some will pressure you to settle the debt right away or be fired.

However, under federal law, an employer can not fire you for a garnishment on a single debt. This means that no matter how often a judgment creditor attaches your earnings, if it is only for one debt, you cannot be fired. But, if two judgment creditors attach your wages with the same employer, whether at the same or different times, you can be fired. Also, if one judgment creditor attaches your wages for two different debts, you can be fired.

Now, what may happen is that even though a judgment creditor attaches your wages for only one debt, your employer gets antsy and wants the matter settled. She knows she cannot fire you because of one attachment, but she may fire you for some phony reason, such as being late to work. If this should happen, see a lawyer right away. If you are poor, legal aid may help you.

We have found, however, that most employers are willing to work with employees who are honestly trying to clear up their problems. It is best to talk with your employer when your wages are being attached and make her understand that you are working hard to settle the matter as soon as possible.

D. Stopping a Wage Attachment

1. Negotiation

Creditors attach your wages because they cannot get money from you any other way. They don't particularly like the paper work involved and are afraid that a wage attachment may result in your filing bankruptcy or perhaps even getting fired. So, they will normally agree to stop an attachment if you make some reasonable offer of payment. It's never too late to begin negotiating with them. They have more clout now, but you can still work out an agreement. Go back and read Chapter 7.

You should also consider contacting Consumer Credit Counselors (see Chapter 3, Section C). They carry considerable weight and can often persuade the judgment creditor to halt the attachment and work out an agreement.

2. Bankruptcy

Filing bankruptcy will end the wage attachment. But before you decide to file, read Chapter 18.

E. Claim of Exemption

Under some circumstances you can keep all of your wages, even the 25%, if you can show that they are really necessary to support you and your family. However, there are several bizarre exceptions to this remedy which should make you stop and think before relying on this device.

For example, if your wages are being snatched because of a debt incurred for a "basic necessity" of life, you cannot use the Claim of Exemption remedy. Why not? Apparently, the legislature feels that if your debt is for a basic needs item, it should be paid off, even if you suffer horrible hardship in the meantime. Also, since these items are not covered by the Claim of Exemption process, merchants will be encouraged to provide them on credit without fear that they won't be able to collect later.

What are these common necessities? The list would probably include rent, food, utilities, most clothes (but not luxury items), medical bills (but not necessarily psychiatrist's bills), and

beds and basic furniture. They would not be:

☐ restaurant bills
☐ veterinary bills
☐ automobilies
☐ motor cycles
☐ garden equipment
☐ fancy furniture
☐ boats
☐ sports equipment
☐ cameras
☐ travel

This exception is particularly confusing since in the next chapter we talk about filing a Claim Of Exemption From Attachment to protect your basic necessities from attachment. In other words, the legislature wants your wages to be available for payment of common necessity debts, but doesn't want the items themselves available. Just remember: You may exempt all your wages from attachment if the debts are not for a common necessity. Conversely, you may be able to exempt most of your basic necessity property from being taken to satisfy the same debt. See Chapter 11.

Additional exceptions are:

■ Withholding orders for child support and alimony obligations;

■ Withholding orders for the payment of state taxes; and

■ Debts owed as wages to another.

Is this difficult to take? Sorry.

Many attorneys feel you should always file your Claim of Exemption, even if the debt is clearly for a "common necessity." They say this because there will be times when the judgment creditor will not challenge your claim and you will win automatically. Also, some judges do not consider whether the debt is for a common necessity--they just see whether you can afford to pay the debt or not.

1. How the Procedure Works

a. You should file your Claim of Exemption as soon as possible after you receive an "earnings withholding order"* from your employer. Your employer must provide you with a copy of this order within 10 days of the time she receives it.

b. After you file your Claim of Exemption and an accompanying "Financial Statement," the judgment creditor is notified and he has 10 days to file a challenge to the claim. Most of the time, he will contest, but sometimes because of the costs, he may decide to abandon it. If the judgment creditor doesn't follow through, your withheld wages will be returned to you.

c. If he does contest it, you will be notified and a hearing date will be set before a judge. The hearing will probably be a week or two later, depending upon the county. Make certain you show up. If you don't, you will lose by default. At the hearing you will have to show that you need your earnings for the support of yourself and/or your family, and that the item on which you owe the money is not a common necessity of life (see Section E above).

d. The judge will hear both sides and then make a ruling. Often she will agree with you that the item is not a common necessity, and that all your earnings are necessary and should be exempt. But sometimes the judge will try to work out a compromise and make you pay something. (There are judges who feel that a debtor should never be allowed to "skip" on his debts.)

e. If you win at the hearing, the judgment creditor must wait at least 100 days from the date the earnings withholding order was first served on your employer, or 60 days from the date of your hearing, whichever is later, before he can attach your wages again. If a compromise results or if you lose, then the judgment creditor can attach your wages in the amount settled on for 90 days or until the debt is paid off.

f. After 90 days, the judgment creditor must wait ten days before he can file a new earnings withholding order. You can then file another Claim of Exemption against the new attachment.

g. You can appeal a court order which denies you a Claim of Exemption. Speak to an attorney or legal aid on how to go about it.

2. Filing Your Claim of Exemption

The procedure for filling out a Claim of Exemption is fairly simple. If you feel confident in yourself, you can probably do it without a lawyer. Judges are getting used to people doing their own Claim of Exemption. However, judges often prefer to deal with lawyers rather than people themselves. So it often happens that if you appear at a Claim of Exemption hearing alone, you will more likely be drawn into a compromise with the judgment creditor than if you have a lawyer representing you. If you have a low income, call legal aid. If you

---

* The law on wage attachment is found in the Code of Civil Procedure Section 706.010 et seq.

intend to do it yourself, here's what you should do.

a. The employer must give you a copy of the "earnings withholding order" she received within 10 days from the day she received it.

b. As soon as you receive it, you should go down to the sheriff, marshal or constable's office to file your Claim of Exemption. There is no time limit on when you must file, but if you want to keep as much as you possibly can, you should file your claim right away. (If for some reason you cannot file until later, the judge has the power to retroactively reduce the amount of wages the judgment creditor can take from you.)

c. The Claim of Exemption for Wage Garnishment [Form 982.5(5)] and the Financial Statement [Form 982.5(5.5)] forms which you need to fill out are in the Appendix to this book. Also, your county sheriff, marshal or constable's office and usually the clerk of the court listed on top of the notice you received will also have the proper forms.

d. You file the original and one copy each of the Claim of Exemption and the Financial Statement with the sheriff, marshal or constable. Make a copy of each for yourself too. If you have trouble filling out the form, ask the clerk at the sheriff, marshal, or constable's office, or at the court, to assist you.

e. Within a couple of weeks, you will be notified in writing whether the judgment creditor intends to contest your claim. If he does, you will also be told of the date of the hearing and the location of the courtroom (called a "department"). Make sure you appear. If you do not, you will lose your claim.

If the judgment creditor does not intend to contest your claim, you will so be notified and have your wages returned to you.

f. On the day of your hearing, come early. Check with the court clerk to be sure you are in the right room. Relax and watch the way the judge handles other cases. (If you are nervous, visit the court a day earlier just to get yourself accustomed to the surroundings.)

g. At the hearing, you will have to prove your claim. You should be prepared to argue that you need your income to support yourself and/or your family. If you have made an unusually high income one month, bring wage stubs and other proof to show that you usually make much less. Also, if you have unusually high medical bills one month, bring proof. The judge is not required to look at these proofs, but she usually will.

Most judges are used to people doing it themselves, so don't be frightened. Tell the judge how serious it would be if you weren't allowed to keep all your income. She may try to draw you into agreeing to pay something, so be prepared. If you're suffering, let the judge know it. If you have kids, bring them along and let them sit in the first row. Remember, the judge is not going to know how much you are hurting unless you show it.

h. Good luck.

3. How Often Can You File?

You can file a Claim of Exemption against a wage attachment any time after you receive the "earnings withholding order." See Section 1(f) above. Once you file your claim, unless your circumstances have changed, you must wait until you receive a new earnings withholding order (usually within 100 days from the last) before you can file another Claim of Exemption.

However, if your circumstances have

changed (for example, you have additional medical expenses or increased support payments, or your rent has gone up, etc.), you can immediately file at any time for another Claim of Exemption.

4. Legislation to Protect People's Rights

If you have only had to read the wage exemption material three times to understand it, you are doing pretty well. Yes, it's needlessly complicated and cumbersome. But you should understand that the complications exist not because they need to, but because creditors want debtors to have to go to so much trouble to exempt their wages that they won't bother. What can you do? Contact your state legislator and request legislation to do away with the unfair procedures which make a person in debt rush to file legal papers in order to keep the money he or she desperately needs.

chapter 11

$ $ $ $ $ $ $

Attachments of Motor Vehicles, Bank Accounts and Other Personal Property

If you have not done so, read Chapter 9.

Besides attaching your wages, the judgment creditor may attach your personal property. Personal property is everything but a house and land. (They are called real property and are discussed in the following chapter.)

Often a debtor does not have much in the way of valuable personal possessions and what she has is exempt; see Section B below. But if she has a fairly valuable car that is paid for, furniture which can easily be resold, such as a stereo component set costing $1,500, or money in the bank, etc., the judgment creditor may decide to come after it. Attachments of furniture are quite rare and only occur when there are extremely valuable items. Attachments of bank accounts and motor vehicles are common. If the judgment creditor does decide to attach, he will send the sheriff or marshal to take the item, have it sold at a public auction, and apply the proceeds of the sale to the debt. The procedure is not much different from a wage attachment, but let's go through it.

A. The Attachment Procedure

1. The judgment creditor has just obtained a judgment against you on the debt.

2. Often immediately, but any time within the next 10 years, he can get an order from the court allowing him to attach your property. This is called a "Writ of Execution."

3. He pays the sheriff a fee and instructs him to attach the asset of yours which is described in the "writ." Since a car is often the most common possession attached, let's use it for our example. Other personal property is treated in a similar way.

4. The sheriff or marshal goes out to your home (or wherever the judgment creditor says your car is located). If you are home, he will explain that he has come to take the car in order to sell it and use the proceeds of the sale to pay off part or all of your debt. If you are not home, he will post the writ on your door.

5. If you do not give the sheriff or marshal the keys, or if you are not home, he will use a master set of his own or hot wire the car. (You can be arrested for interfering with the sheriff or marshal, so stay cool.)

6. The sheriff or marshal will take the car to a garage for storage and wait 10 days.

7. If you do not file a Claim of Exemption on the car (see Section D) within that time, the vehicle will be put up for public sale.

8. The sale is usually held a week or two later, depending upon the county. The proceeds of the sale will be used to pay off the debt, though the sheriff will first take out costs, towing, and storage charges.

B. Exempt Assets

We mentioned in Chapter 9 that the state has adopted legislation to protect you from losing all your possessions to the judgment creditor. You should not have to be without certain basic items, merely because you owe money on a debt. These items are known as "exempt assets" and most of them are personal property. Here is a list.

1. Household Items

These include the following:

☐ Household furnishings
☐ Appliances
☐ Clothing
☐ Other personal effects

The law provides that these items are exempt if they are "ordinarily and reasonably necessary" to and personally used by the debtor and members of her family. In determining whether an item is "ordinarily and reasonably necessary," the court will consider 1) the extent to which the particular item is ordinarily found in a household and 2) whether the particular item has extraordinary value as compared to the value of items of the same type found in other households. If an item is found to be of extraordinary value, it is not exempt. However, when it is sold to pay off the debt to the judgment creditor, a portion of the proceeds from the sale is exempt so that the debtor may purchase an ordinary replacement of the item (providing the court determines that a replacement is reasonably necessary). The actual amount that is exempt from the proceeds and goes to the debtor is determined by the court.

For example, if the debtor owns an extremely valuable piano, it could be attached and sold, but a portion of the proceeds from the sale would be returned to the debtor so that she could purchase a more reasonably valued piano (assuming the judge felt that a piano was reasonably necessary to the debtor).

Courts are pretty lenient in finding that almost all furniture and clothing is necessary. You should always file a Claim of Exemption on any clothing, furniture or appliance.

2. Motor Vehicles

You can keep one or more motor vehicles, such as an automobile, truck or motorcycle, where the amount of your equity in the vehicle(s) totals no more than $1,200. This means you could keep any number of vehicles if the collective value of your ownership is less than $1,200, but cannot keep your only car if your ownership is worth more than $1,200.

Your equity or ownership value is measured by the difference between the car's sale value and the amount you would be entitled to keep after the sale. If your car could be sold for $4,000, but $3,000 of that would have to go to repay a loan secured by the car, your equity is only $1,000 and the car will be exempted. If you owe money on the car but are unsure of how much,

check with your creditor--he'll be sure to know. If you own the car outright, then your equity is equal to its sale value.

If your equity in the vehicle(s) is more than $1,200, the creditor, through the sheriff or bankruptcy trustee, can legally take it, sell it at a public sale, and apply any amount of the proceeds over $1,200 to your debts. The first $1,200, however, belongs to you and cannot be attached for 90 days or at all if you invest it in exempt property within that period (including another car with less than $1,200 equity).

3. Tools of the Trade or Business

Tools, implements, instruments, materials, uniforms, furnishings, books, equipment, one commercial motor vehicle, one vessel, and other personal property reasonably necessary to and actually used by the debtor or the debtor's spouse in a trade, business or profession are exempt up to an aggregate value of $2,500. In order for the commercial vehicle under this section to be exempt, the debtor cannot have exempted a vehicle which would be reasonably and adequately used in the debtor's trade, business or profession under the vehicle exemption section (see Section 2, above).

In finding items which are used in your business, trade or profession, don't necessarily limit yourself to the obvious. Be imaginative.

As is the case with the vehicle exception, if your tools are taken because they exceed $2,500, you will receive $2,500 to replace them with.

4. Jewelry, Heirlooms, Works of Art

Jewelry, heirlooms and works of art are exempt to the extent that their aggregate value does not exceed $2,500. This amount is separate from and in addition to the other exemptions discussed in this chapter.

5. Health Aids

Health aids reasonably necessary to enable the debtor, spouse or dependent to work or sustain health are exempt. Health aids include prosthetic and orthopedic appliances, as well as a wheel chair or even an air conditioner for a person afflicted with asthma. However, they would not include a portable swimming pool used merely because its use is necessary to sustain good health.

6. Materials for Repair or Improvement of a Dwelling

Material which is about to be applied to the repair or improvement of the debtor's principal place of residence (or the dwelling of the debtor's spouse where the debtor and spouse are separated) is exempt up to $1,000.

7. Insurance

Life insurance policies to an aggregate loan value of $4,000 are exempt. If the debtor is married, each spouse is entitled to a separate exemption and the exemptions of the spouses may be combined. Benefits from life insurance policies are exempt to the extent reasonably necessary for the support of the debtor and family.

8. Pensions

Funds and benefits from public (CCP. 704.110) and private (CCP.704.115) retirement systems are exempt from all judgments except those for child and spousal support. IRA and Keogh plans are exempt only to the extent necessary to support the debtor and his/her family at retirement. (CCP.704.115)

9. Public Benefits

The following public benefits are exempt: Unemployment benefits, disability benefits, benefits paid by a union due to a labor dispute, workers' compensation, public assistance, relocation benefits, and financial aid to students.

10. Social Security Payments

Social security payments are exempt. In addition, you can keep $500 on deposit in an account in which social security payments are directly deposited.

11. Other Items

There are other specialized items which are also exempt. These include funds in an inmate's trust account up to a value of $1,000; a family burial plot; personal injury causes of action (lawsuits) and damages, and wrongful death actions and damages to the extent necessary to support the debtor and family (or if paid in installments, then a minimum of 75 percent is exempt); public employee vacation credits; disability and health insurance benefits, and business licenses.

Also, bank accounts or cash which can be traced to an exempt asset (such as earnings paid during the previous thirty days, disability, unemployment, pensions) are exempt.

The following list sets out the exemptions and the appropriate Code of Civil Procedure Section (be sure to check the supplement in back of the code book to see whether any new items have been added or revisions have been made):

TYPE OF ASSET	C.C.P.
Motor Vehicles	704.010
Household items	704.020
Materials for repair or improvement of a residence	704.030
Jewelry, heirlooms, art	704.040
Health aids	704.050
Tools of the trade or business	704.060
Earnings paid (also see Chapter 10)	704.070
Social Security deposits	704.080
Inmates trust account	704.090
Life insurance	704.100
Public retirement benefits	704.110
Public employee vacation credits	704.113
Private retirement benefits	704.115
Unemployment benefits, disability benefits, strike benefits	704.120
Health or disability insurance benefits	704.130
Personal injury damages	704.140
Wrongful death damages	704.150
Workers' compensation	704.160
Public assistance	704.170
Relocation benefits	704.180
Student financial aid	704.190
Cemetary plot	704.200
Bank accounts and cash traced to an exempt asset	703.080
Business licenses	695.060

NOTE ON EXEMPTIONS AND SECURED DEBTS: There is this exception to the exemption law: If you owe money on a secured debt and the secured creditor has gotten a judgment against you for it, you cannot claim that item as an exemption, although it would otherwise qualify as one. (A secured debt is where the creditor has legal title to the item until you make all the payments on it; see Chapter 5.)

Here is an example: You buy a sofa bed for $600 and the dealer keeps legal title to it until you pay it off. You stop making payments and the dealer gets a judgment against you for the amount you still owe. The dealer then can attach the sofa bed and you cannot claim an exemption for it (even though it would be a valid Claim of Exemption against any other creditor trying to attach it, such as a doctor or credit card company). To keep the sofa bed, you would have to continue making payments on it.

If an item is legally owned by a creditor under a security agreement, it can still be grabbed and sold by another creditor. In such a case, the secured creditor will be entitled to receive the proceeds of the sale up to what is owed under the security agreement, with the second creditor only getting what's left. For this reason, any item owned by you under a security agreement will probably not be seized by another creditor unless your equity in it is enough to result in the second creditor making some money from the sale.

C. Turning Non-Exempt Assets into Exempt Ones

If you have an asset which is not exempt, especially money, you would do well to convert it to an asset which is exempt before the judgment creditor has a chance to attach it. This is not only sensible, but legal. Here are a few examples:

1. You have a very expensive saxophone and are a carpenter. Sell the sax and use the money to buy yourself some more tools that you need for your work. (As long as the total sale value of all your equipment is below $2,500, you're safe.)

2. You have a valuable collection of stamps, coins, or guns. Sell it and use the money as a down payment on a home and homestead it (see Chapter 12).

3. You have two cars; your equity in one car is $1,200, in the other it is $1,000. Since combined they exceed the $1,200 limit, sell the $1,200 vehicle and use the money to pay the dentist for fixing your children's teeth.

D. Filing Your Claim of Exemption

After the creditor gets a judgment against you, he or she then obtains a "Writ of Execution" from the court clerk. The creditor takes this writ to the sheriff or marshal and directs them to attach some item of yours in the hope

that it will be used to help pay off the debt. Where the creditor goes after an item which is exempt under the law you can file a "Claim of Exemption" to protect it.

The procedure for filing a Claim of Exemption is fairly simple. If you feel confident in yourself, you can probably do it without a lawyer. Judges are getting used to people doing their own exemption claims. However, judges often prefer to deal with lawyers rather than people themselves. So it often happens that if you appear at a Claim of Exemption hearing alone, you will more likely be drawn into a compromise with the judgment creditor than if you have a lawyer representing you. If you have a low income, call legal aid. If you intend to do it yourself, here's what you should do:

1. You must file your claim with the sheriff or marshal within 10 days from the date the notice of the attachment was served on you. You should file your Claim of Exemption with one copy as soon as you are notified of the attachment. Also, call the sheriff or marshal's office and ask them from what date they begin counting off the 10 days.

2. Turn to the Appendix and locate the Claim of Exemption form for Enforcement of Judgment (it says [Not For Wage Garnishment] at the top). This form can also be obtained from your sheriff or marshal's office, or from the court clerk of the court listed on the paper served on you.

3. You will have to fill in the proper code section in the Claim of Exemption form. A list of California Code of Civil Procedure exemptions is included in Section B, above. It would be a good idea to go to your local law library and check the supplement in the back of the appropriate Code of Civil Procedure volume to check on any recent revisions.

4. You must deliver your Claim of Exemption and copy to the sheriff or marshal's office within the 10 days. If you wish to mail the papers, call first to make sure the sheriff or marshal will accept them by mail. If they will, they will probably require that the copies reach the office within the 10-day period.

5. Within a week or two, you will be notified whether the judgment creditor intends to contest your claim. If so, you will be told of the date of the hearing and the courtroom (called a "department"). Make sure you appear. If you do not, you will lose your claim.

If the judgment creditor does not contest your claim, the property will be released back to you.

6. On the day of the hearing, come early. Check with the court clerk to be sure you are in the right room. Relax and watch the way the judge handles other cases. (If you are nervous, visit the court a day earlier to get yourself accustomed to the surroundings.)

7. Be prepared to establish your right to your property under the law. If they are the tools of your trade or your mobile home, for example, bring an expert witness who can testify to the fact that the value does not exceed your exemption amount. Be sure to bring whatever papers or other evidence you need (savings passbook, etc.).

8. Good luck.

—————▽—————

chapter 12

$ $ $ $ $ $ $

Protecting Your
Home and Land

If you have not done so, read Chapter 9.

Judgment creditors usually do not care how they get the money, they just want to get it. And they want it in the easiest way, expending the least effort. That is why they usually go after your wages first. But they may decide that an even more effective route would be to attach your home if you own one. They know that your home is probably your most valuable possession and you don't want to lose it. It often happens that merely by beginning the attachment procedure against a debtor's unprotected home, a creditor frightens the debtor into figuring out some way to pay off the debt immediately and save the home.

A. Homestead Protection

Under the California homestead laws, your equity in your dwelling place is protected up to a certain amount. At present, the legislature has protected ownership equity in a dwelling up to $45,000 for a married couple and a family unit (two or more people related to certain degrees). Individuals 65 years of age or over, or people phyically or mentally disabled and unable to work, are entitled to $55,000 in protection. The protection is $30,000 for all other persons. Two unrelated individuals can jointly own a house and each one is entitled to an exemption of $30,000 (or $55,000 if he or she is over 65 or disabled).

In some cases your home can be sold so long as you are provided with your exemption amount; in most others, however, your home is safe from a forced sale to satisfy your debts. There are three basic ways the homestead law works, depending on whether:

1. You have filed a Declaration of Homestead;

2. There is no declaration filed on your home but it consists of real estate (the way most homes do); or

3. Your dwelling is classified as personal property, such as a boat or motor home.

If your home is situated on land, skip Section B and begin reading at Section C. If, on the other hand, you live in a boat or motor home (registered with the Department of Motor Vehicles), Section B is for you.

SOME GENERAL EXCEPTIONS: The homestead laws do not protect you in the following situations:

■ Collection of taxes by state or federal government.

■ Foreclosure proceedings by the holder of a mortgage or deed of trust.

B. Personal Property Dwellings

Dwellings classified as personal property, such as a boat or motor home, are protected up to the statutory amount under the homestead laws, if:

1. You are living in it when the creditor files his or her judgment with the county recorder; and

2. You are still living in it at the time your homestead exemption is determined in court.

Unlike the situation if your dwelling is connected with land, however, you must file a Claim of Exemption if your dwelling is attached and you want your full protection.

While the judgment creditor is entitled to force a sale of your personal property dwelling, regardless of what your equity in it is, this will almost never occur UNLESS your equity substantially exceeds the amount of your homestead exemption. For example, if you are a married couple and your equity in your houseboat is $35,000, a forced sale would result in your getting your $35,000 and the creditor getting nothing. This assumes, of course, that your creditor does not own a security interest in the boat.

If the judgment creditor wants to sell your personal property dwelling to satisfy a judgment, you will be served with a Writ of Possession by a sheriff or marshal, informing you that your home has been seized. To protect your homesteaded equity, and in most cases discourage the sale, you must file a Claim of Exemption. This will be the same form that we showed you in Chapter 11. As we mentioned in that chapter, it must be filled in with appropriate references to the Code of Civil Procedure and filed with the sheriff or marshal within 10 days after the Writ of Possession was served on you. The Code sections applicable to your situation are C.C.P. 703.520, 704.710, and 704.730.

If the creditor wants to contest your Claim of Exemption, you will receive a Notice of Hearing. You should attend that hearing and be prepared to prove, through witnesses and documents, that you were residing in the dwelling at the time the judgment was filed and that you are still living there. You will also need to prove your entitlement to the particular sum you are claiming ($30,000, $45,000, $50,000). For more detail on how to handle this procedure, see HOMESTEAD YOUR HOUSE, Nolo Press (see back of this book).

C. Real Property Dwellings

In most cases, a home in which you have an ownership interest will be a house, condominium, cottage, or mobile home permanently attached to land. These types of real property dwellings are automatically protected up to the statutory amount so long as you are living in them when the creditor files the judgment with the county recorder and at the time a court hearing is held with respect to your homestead.

If a creditor wants to have your real property dwelling sold, he or she must first apply to a court for an order permitting the sale. You will be notified of the hearing and must attend if you want to claim your homestead amount.* At the hearing you will have the burden of showing that you were and are residing in the dwelling and that you are entitled to the amount you are claiming (e.g., $30,000, $45,000, $55,000).

Assuming you establish your entitlement to the homestead exemption, your dwelling cannot be sold unless the creditor establishes that a sale would produce more money than a combination of your exemption, any existing mortgages and liens on the house, and the normal costs of sale. For example, assume your

---

* If you had good reasons for not attending the hearing, there is a way to get a second chance. See HOMESTEAD YOUR HOUSE, Nolo Press, on how to do this.

house could be sold for $100,000. If the amount still due on your mortgage (usually called a "deed of trust" in California) is $50,000, your homestead exemption is $45,000, and the expected costs of sale would be 6%, or $6,000. The total of these three items would be $101,000. Since this amount is greater than the sale amount, the dwelling could not be sold. If, however, you own a $100,000 house free and clear, it may be sold, since the amount realized from the sale would greatly exceed the other three items.

D. Homesteading Your Dwelling

Although you are automatically protected under the homestead laws up to the statutory amount, it is possible to declare a homestead on your real property dwelling and gain some additional protection by merely filing a simple form with the county recorder before someone files a judgment against you. This procedure, complete with the necessary forms, is available in HOMESTEAD YOUR HOUSE.

The homestead protection is identical in amount to what you get under your exemption claim--namely, $45,000 for a married couple, or a single person head of household, $30,000 for a single person, and $55,000 for a person over 65 or a person who is mentally or physically disabled and unable to work.* It covers all real property dwellings.

As with the automatic homestead, you must be living in your home when the judgment is filed against your proper-

---

* The Court of Appeals has held that a homeowner is automatically entitled to the amount of the homestead exemption in effect at the time an attempted enforcement of judgment takes place rather than the amount in effect at the time the homestead was filed. This means that, if the homestead limit gets raised after you've placed one on your home, you don't have to run down and file a new one. The law will automatically consider you covered by the new higher amount.

ty. But, there are considerable advantages to filing a Declaration of Homestead. These are:

1. A declared homestead survives the death of a judgment debtor in regard to a spouse or family provided that such surviving person is living in the house upon the judgment debtor's death and inherits some part of the property.

2. A homestead protects your equity in a house from debts incurred prior to buying a house as long as the homestead declaration was filed before a judgment lien was filed against the house. The automatic homestead law does not.

3. If you sell a homesteaded house and your homestead declaration was filed prior to the filing of any judgment liens, you can get your money and have six months to put it into another house.* If you have not homesteaded, and judgment liens have been filed against your home, Section 704.720 (the automatic homestead law) would seem to give you the same right to get your money out of one house and into another, but in practice it does not. Title companies interpret the law in a conservative fashion and will not establish clear title until you have paid off all the liens. This means that it will be difficult, or more likely impossible, to sell a non-homesteaded house unless you pay off the judgment liens.

4. At the hearing to determine whether your house should be sold, the creditor has the burden of disproving your exemption, unlike the automatic homestead situation where you have the burden of claiming it.

5. In several other areas of the law, such as bankruptcy, divorce, and even with regard to the definition of "dwelling house," it is not clear that an exemption under Section 704.730 gives as good protection as a homestead.

Remember, you can only homestead your

---

* However, any mechanics' liens on the property must be paid first.

house before the creditor gets a judgment and records it with the county recorder. You can file for it while you are being sued. Homesteading will not protect you from judgments filed against you before you filed your Declaration of Homestead.

E. If Your Home Has Been Attached and Sold

If your home has been attached by a creditor and sold at a forced sale, you may still have a chance to get it back. Consult a lawyer.

F. Property Taxes

California law allows you to be delinquent in your property taxes for up to five years before the property is taken and sold for back taxes. Here's an example:

If you do not pay your 84-85 property taxes (taxes run on a fiscal year, July 1-June 30), then on July 1, 1985 you will be considered delinquent. But not until July 1, 1990 will your property be "tax deeded" to the county and prepared for public auction the following October. In October, 1990 you would lose your property if you still hadn't paid the taxes.

You can pay delinquent property taxes any time during the five years. However, very high interest rates are added on for late payment.

If five years have passed and your property is taken by the county, you have additional time to recover it. Between July 1 and the auction in October, you can redeem your property if you pay the full amount.

There is another angle you should consider, though, when you don't pay property taxes. In some cases, the mortgager will pay the taxes and then go against you for them. This can happen any time within the five years.

1. Are You Buying Property?

Property taxes run against property, not against people. So be careful when you purchase property. If there is a tax delinquency on it and you purchase the property, you are responsible for the delinquency. If a title search is performed in connection with your purchase, you will be informed of any existing tax delinquencies. If no title search is being done, however, and you're handling your own escrow, we suggest you read ALL ABOUT ESCROW, Robinson, Express Press.

2. Senior Citizens' Property Tax Relief

Senior citizens 62 years or older, whose income is $24,000 or less, can have their property taxes, special assessments and other charges and fees deferred.* The amounts would be deducted from the value of their property after they die. Rev. & Tax Code Section 20581-86 and 20601 et.seq. For more information, call the State Controller's Office at [800] 952-5661.

---

* This figure is $24,000, except for people who filed and qualified in 1983, in which case, the limit is $34,000.

G. Refinancing and Second Mortgages

1. Refinancing

Ten years ago, Steven Mitchell bought a $100,000 home. He paid $20,000 down and assumed a $80,000 mortgage payable over 25 years. He has paid off $20,000 to date. Today he is in debt and needs money. To get it, he can "refinance" his home. He would take a new mortgage (possibly again $80,000) on his home, use it to pay off what is left on his present mortgage ($60,000), and pocket the difference ($20,000).**

Turning in your equity in your home for cash is sometimes a good idea. But if you intend to do it, consider the following:

a. It will extend the time period in which you have to pay off the mortgage and make it harder for you to ever own your home "free and clear."

b. If interest rates are high, it will cost you more to pay off your home than if you continued paying at the rate you got at the time you took the original mortgage.

c. Always go to a bank or credit union first. Be sure to check with the people who have the original mortgage and find out how much of a pre-payment penalty you incur by paying off the mortgage ahead of time. Shop around for the best terms.

d. If the equity in your home is climbing above the dollar value of the homestead exemption, you can refinance your home and bring that equity down, so your creditors will not have anything to attach.

** With today's inflated prices of homes, Steven's old home would probably be worth around $200,000. Thus, he could refinance his home for a lot more (perhaps even up to $140,000) and walk away with a bundle.

2. Second Mortgages and Deeds of Trust

In our example above, Steven could also go to a second mortgage company (they often have the word "plan" as a part of their name), borrow $20,000, and mortgage his house as a security for the loan. This would be his "second mortgage," or "second deed of trust," as they're often called.

People often take second mortgages rather than refinancing their home. Usually this is a bad choice. Whenever possible, you should refinance. It will save you a lot of headaches and possible misery.

Here's how second mortgage companies operate:

■ Most real estate "plans" which offer second mortgages are nothing more than "mortgage brokers" who use the money of rich people who want to invest in high interest paying loans. The brokers rarely invest their own money.

■ The interest rate is 12%-18% and there are a number of additional charges, like "finder's fees" or commissions, title insurance, title search, credit investigations, and escrow and recording fees. This can all total up to a whopping 29% of the loan.

■ On loans for three years or more, many of these companies provide for the final installment payment to be much greater than the preceding installment payments. This final payment is called

a "balloon payment." Often people are unable to make this payment and so are forced to refinance and again pay all those costs, commissions, expenses, etc. So watch out.

■ These groups advertise that they are not interested in your credit. Sounds attractive, but it isn't. Remember, you put up your home as security. And if you miss a payment--zoom--they swoop down and take it from you. They often hope that people will not repay. They make their big profits in foreclosing on your home and milking all the equity you have in it.

■ Some collection agencies are in league with these "plans." When you owe collection agencies money, they may suggest you take a second mortgage with a "plan" which they name. Watch out. They may have a kickback deal going with the plan. Don't take the "friendly" advice of the collection agency. They are not your friends. Check for the best refinancing or second mortgage deal on your own.

a. Checking Out a "Plan"

If your bank or credit union will not refinance your home and you need to go to one of these "plans" to get a second mortgage, call the Better Business Bureau. Ask them on which second mortgage "plans" they have received complaints. Don't go to these. Some brokers are more reputable than others. Check around.

b. Making a Complaint

If you have any trouble with any of these plans, or brokers or salesmen, contact the Department of Real Estate office that covers your area. (Let the plan know that you are complaining.) There are offices in Sacramento, San Francisco, Fresno, Los Angeles, and San Diego. The addresses and phone numbers are listed below. You can make a complaint in person (bring all important papers with you), call and ask them to send you a complaint form, or send them a letter including the name of the company, its address, the names of the people with whom you dealt, the dates and the details of the incident.

- SACRAMENTO
  1719 24th Street
  Sacramento, CA 95816
  (916) 445-5741

- LOS ANGELES
  Room 8107
  107 S.Broadway
  Los Angeles, CA 90012
  (213) 620-5903

- FRESNO
  Room 3070
  2550 Mariposa Street
  Fresno, CA 93721
  (209) 445-5009

- SAN FRANCISCO
  185 Berry, Suite 5816
  San Francisco, CA 94107
  (415) 557-3953

- SAN DIEGO
  Room 5008
  1350 Front St.
  San Diego, CA 92101
  (619) 237-7345

- SANTA ANA
  28 Civic Center
    Plaza, Room 324
  Santa Ana, CA 92701
  (717) 558-4491

c. Recovery Fund

California also provides a "Recovery Fund" which will reimburse a person for money he has lost as a result of some fraudulent act by a licensed real estate broker. However, you must first get a judgment against the broker and be unable to collect on the judgment. Contact the Department of Real Estate or an attorney for assistance.

chapter 13

$ $ $ $ $ $ $

Orders of Examination

What if your judgment creditor doesn't know what possessions you have, or where you work, or if you have a bank account? How is he to attach your assets? Or what if he knows where you work and attaches your wages, but you file a Claim of Exemption and win? Which one of your possessions would be the most valuable for him to go after next?

Well, a judgment creditor has various schemes of finding these things out. If the judgment is entered against you in Small Claims Court, you must file a "Judgment Debtors' Statement of Assets" within 35 days. In Municipal or Superior Court, he can ask you about your assets and income in person, and you must respond. This procedure is called an Order For Appearance and Examination (usually shortened to Order of Examination).

A. How an Order of Examination Works

Under the law, the judgment creditor can go to the court and ask the judge to issue an Order of Examination requiring you to appear before the judge to answer, under oath, questions from the judgment creditor or his lawyer about your assets. If you receive such an order, you had better appear on the date and at the place indicated. If you do not, you can be held in contempt of court and face arrest. The only restriction on the judgment creditor is that he cannot require you to appear more often than once every four months.

B. Received an Order But Cannot Appear?

If you receive an Order of Examination but cannot afford to take time off from work or for some other reason cannot appear, call the judgment creditor or his attorney and explain your situation. Express to him your willingness to answer his questions over the phone or perhaps in person at another time. Since all the judgment creditor really wants is the information, in most instances he will be satisfied to get it over the phone if he feels that you are being cooperative and honest.

If you come to an agreement with a judgment creditor to answer his questions on the phone or at another time, ask him to send you a note verifying that you need not appear at the hearing date set in the Order of Examination. It is also wise to send him a note, with a copy to the court with the court number written on the top, and keep a copy of it for yourself. An example follows.

NOTE: Never take any money with you to an Order of Examination. The creditor can ask you to empty your pockets or purse and can take any money in your possession.

```
                                  181 Cottage Avenue
                                  Yreka, California
                                  May 17, 19__

         Court No.   [this number appears on
                      the order served on you]

Mervyn Loya
610 Eugene Street
Redding, California

Dear Mr. Loya,

   I am writing to confirm our phone conversa-
tion of May 15, 19__.

   On that day, I answered all the questions
you asked me on the state of my assets and
employment. You were satisfied with my cooper-
ation and stated that I need not appear in
court on May 25, 19__ to answer to the Order of
Examination you had issued to me.

                            Very truly yours,

                            Julie Buttress
```

chapter 14

$ $ $ $ $ $ $

Credit Cards

A. An American Folk Tale

A number of years ago, Bank of America issued thousands of Bank Americards to people in Northern California. Seemingly, if you had a charge account, a savings account, or a checking account, you received a card. A few months later, collection agencies were called in to repossess the cards of and collect on the many non-paying accounts.

Sounds like the old B. of A. took a beating, doesn't it? But you know better than that. Bank of America wouldn't be the largest bank in the country if they didn't know exactly what they were doing. As one representative of the Bank told a friend, it was cheaper for them to just mail out the cards and take the loss on the bad debts than to send

out applications, check credit reports on each person, and process all the forms.

Doing it their way, they accomplished their purpose in weeding out the bad accounts at the least cost. In addition, they succeeded in fulfilling the goal of every credit card company whether a bank, oil company, department store or airline, namely: to get everyone to carry their particular brand of credit card; for credit cards are there to be used. The fact that lots of people got hopelessly in debt using credit cards that they never asked for and did not fully understand was just one of those unavoidable costs of doing business.

Credit cards are nothing other than very expensive loans. The interest rates on money not paid back within a given time period (usually 30 days) is around 18% a year.* The companies profit on the fact that most people do not pay off their credit card debt within that given time period. If they did, the companies would soon go out of existence. In effect, credit card companies want you to stay in debt, and some have begun charging people extra for paying their bills on time.

B. Receiving Unrequested Cards

The law has changed and now no card can be legally issued except in response to a request or application. If a company sends you a new unrequested card, it must take full responsibility for its use (Civil Code Section 1747.05 and 15 U.S.C. Section 1642).

C. Stolen or Lost Credit Cards

State law limits any loss you would incur if your card were lost or stolen. If you notify the company or bank which issued the card within a reasonable time after you discovered (or should have discovered) the loss or theft, you are not liable for any unauthorized use of your card. In no case can you be liable for more than $50 (Civil Code Section 1747.10, 15 USC Section 1643).**

---

* Not all states allow credit card companies to charge the outrageous interest of 18% or more a year.

** A California appeals court has upheld an award of $150,000 to a woman against a bank which had refused to cancel unauthorized charges made on the woman's credit card after she reported the card stolen. The bank was also found to have violated the law by giving her a poor credit rating. YOUNG V. BANK OF AMERICA NATIONAL TRUST AND SAVINGS ASSOC., 141 Cal.App.3d 108 (1983).

You can notify the credit card company by telephone, telegram, letter or postcard. If you decide to send a letter, keep a copy for your records. A sample letter you can use follows. To find the address of the company, just look on the postage-paid, addressed envelope or postcard they were required to send you with your card. If you have lost the envelope, look at any of the statements you have received from them in previous months, or look in your nearest metropolitan phone book. (Remember, a phone call is just as good as a letter, and most credit card companies have toll-free "800" numbers. You can call many of the major bank credit card offices 24 hours a day, seven days a week.)

2147 Porky Street
Davis, California
February 27, 19__

Shortage Oil Company
Credit Card Department
1 Main Street
Potato, California

Dear Sir:

This is to inform you that I lost my Shortage Oil Company credit card yesterday, February 26, 19__ somewhere in the vicinity of Rose and Milvia Streets in Davis.

I understand that under the law this letter serves as reasonably timely notice to you and that I am not liable for any unauthorized use of this card.

Sincerely,

Michael Pitre

D. Problems with Credit Card Purchases

If you buy goods or services with your credit card and the items turn out to be defective, you may refuse to pay for them if the seller refuses to replace or repair or otherwise correct the problem. Just notify the credit card company why you are withholding payment (15 U.S.C. Section 1666i., Civil Code Section 1747.90).

There are no limitations on this right if the seller is owned or operated by the creditor-credit card company, as would be the case with a department store card, a gas company card, or an airline card, or if the creditor mailed you an advertisement for the item.

However, if it is a third party or bank credit card, such as BankAmericard, MasterCard, or American Express, your purchase must have been more than $50 and been made within your state or within 100 miles of your home.

NOTE: See Chapter 4, Section J for a discussion on discrimination in credit and credit cards.

E. Billing Errors

If you feel there is an error in your statement, your right to obtain satisfaction has greatly improved (15 U.S.C. 1666). No more need you be frustrated by computers ignoring your complaint.

Begin by writing on a separate sheet of paper, not on the bill, 1) your name and account number, 2) an explanation of the believed error, and 3) the dollar amount of the believed error. Send it to the address given by the company for inquiries. Don't include your copy of the sales slip or other document unless you have a duplicate. The creditor must

receive your notice within 60 days after the bill was mailed to you. See the sample letter below.

---

211 Judge Dee Drive
Fairfax, California
August 20, 19__

Big State Bank
1 State Plaza
San Anselmo, California

Dear People:

I wish to advise you of an error I believe you made in my MasterCard statement.

My name is Robert Van Gulik, my account number is X201KJ. On March 25, 19__, I purchased with my MasterCard two roundtrip tickets on Blue Airlines to Spokane, Washington, for $300. I lost the tickets a few days later and phoned the airlines for a duplicate set.

The charge for the first set of tickets appeared last month in my statement from you. My billing statement this month includes the charge for the second, duplicate set of tickets. Since I only used one set of the tickets, I should not be charged for both of them.

I understand that under the law, you must acknowledge receipt of this letter within 30 days unless you correct this billing error before then, and that within 90 days you must correct the error or explain why you believe the amount to be correct.

Sincerely,

Robert Van Gulik

Now the burden falls on the credit card company. They must acknowledge receipt of your letter within 30 days, unless they correct the billing within that time. Within 90 days after receiving your complaint, the company must either correct the mistake or explain why they believe the bill to be accurate.

IMPORTANT: If the credit card company does not comply with the 30- and 90-day requirements or with any of the other rules mentioned here, you may keep the disputed amount up to $50, whether or not an error had been made.

During the 90 days, or until the company comes up with an explanation, they cannot threaten or take any collection action against you for the disputed amount, though periodic statements may be sent to you. Nor can the amount be reported to a credit bureau or to other creditors as being delinquent.

If the creditor's explanation isn't satisfactory, you may notify them in writing within 10 days that you still refuse to pay. If they then report your delinquency to credit bureaus or other creditors, they must also tell them that you do not believe you owe the money. They must also let you know to whom the reports were made. Once the matter is resolved, the company must notify the credit bureau and other creditors of the resolution. (See Chapter 4 on credit bureaus if you don't know how these outfits work.)

Under the law, if your complaint has not been worked out, whether it was a billing error or because of a defective item (part D above), you can sue the creditor for $100 plus attorneys' fees. If the creditor is local, this suit could be brought in Small Claims Court.

F. Overcharging Your Limit

Many credit cards have a dollar limit on your spending. For example, if your limit is $1,200 and you've used it up, you are not supposed to go out and make any further purchases.

Merchants also have a limit. But theirs works the other way. They must call the credit card company for approval on purchases larger than a certain dollar amount. This amount, known as a "floor limit" differs with different kinds of merchants. If a customer purchases something for a dollar amount beneath that limit, the merchant will be reimbursed by the bank, even if the customer fails to pay. If the purchase is above that limit and the debtor doesn't pay, the merchant will be reimbursed only if he first checks with the central office to okay the purchase.

When you go over your limit, the credit card company may get uptight. It depends upon whether you have been making payments regularly or not. Remember, they want you to use their card so they can get the interest. Unless you've been missing payments, they will probably leave you alone. Of course, if you miss payments they will call or write and ask that you not use your card until you bring the balance below your limit.

chapter 15

$ $ $ $ $ $ $

Student Loans

Until recently, student loans were basically the same as any other loan. That is, the college, bank, or government would act in much the same way as any other creditor or collection agency when it came to collecting their money. The bottom line on these actions was that a court judgment had to be obtained before the money could legally be collected. However, this bottom line changed dramatically.

Under a federal statute,* the Internal Revenue Service is now authorized under certain circumstances to deduct the amount of delinquent student loan payments from a taxpayer's income tax refund. This authority arises when a federally-insured student loan is turned back to the federal government (as discussed in Section B) and the agency responsible for the loan notifies the IRS of the delinquency. The person owing the debt is then given notice of the proposed tax refund deduction by the agency insuring the loan, and provided an opportunity to argue either that the payments are not past due, or are not legally enforceable (e.g., the statute of limitations has run, or for some other reason). If neither point is established to the agency's satisfaction, the IRS is instructed to make

the deduction up to the full amount of the delinquency.

The rest of this chapter discusses student loans on the premise that a court action is necessary to collect them. This continues to be the primary method of collection. For those of you whose tax refund is being placed in jeopardy, our discussion of the statute of limitations in Section F applies to your situation as well. That is, if you can convince the agency that part or all of your delinquency is barred by the statute of limitations (i.e., not legally enforceable), such sums should not be recaptured through tax refund deductions (31 U.S.C.A. 3720A).

A. Bank Loans

The government sponsors a federally-insured student loan program in which the bank lends the money, but the government guarantees its payment.* It is called the Guaranteed Student Loan Program and works like this:

---

* A federal law (50 USC Section 462) requires that young men register for the draft in order to receive loans and other financial aid. The law was found constitutional by the United States Supreme Court in July 1984. SELECTIVE SERVICE SYSTEM V. MINNESOTA PUBLIC INTEREST RESEARCH GROUP (1984) 104 S.Ct. 3348.

The bank lends you the money.* You have no obligation to start paying it back until six months after graduation or after you withdraw from school.** The federal government allows you to be a half-time student and still maintain your student status. Many banks, however, require you to follow a full-time course program to keep your student status, so check with your bank to see whether half-time is sufficient.

During the six-month grace period, you are sent a notice to make contact with the bank to arrange a repayment schedule. If you do not answer their letters, the bank will try other ways to contact you. But, essentially, the bank does not really care much whether you repay the loan or not. The reason for this mellowness is that if after three to four months you still haven't made any payments, the bank just turns the debt over to a state guaranty agency or to the federal Department of Education and asks for its money. The bank hasn't lost anything except future interest, and at 8%, that isn't very much.*** They can do much better using the money for other loans that pay higher interest.

Over the years, the energy the Federal Department of Education has put into its efforts to collect delinquent educational loan payments has waxed and waned. At one time, the Department relied on nearly 1,000 full-time bill collectors to pursue people who defaulted on their student loans. At other times, this staff has been virtually eliminated. Currently, the Department claims a renewed effort to press collections.

The Department of Education obtains current addresses of people who do not pay their student loans by using computers to cross check delinquent accounts against IRS information. And, as we saw in the introduction to this chapter, federal tax refunds may now, under certain circumstances, be intercepted to repay student loans without the need for traditional collection techniques.

B. College Loans

Most college loans are National Direct Student Loans (NDSL). There are also some student loans from private or university sources. The college loans generally work as follows:

For most loans, there is a nine-month grace period after graduation or withdrawal. A letter to work out a repayment schedule is sent out during this period. If after the nine months pass no payment plan is set up, there is an additional waiting period of three to six months. The length of time depends upon the contacts they have with you, how in need the college is of the money, and how good your excuses are.

After this period passes and the college feels frustrated with your account. it will do one of the following:

1. Turn the loan over to the school's General Counsel's office for possible litigation. (The college may also notify the local credit bureaus that your student loan account has become delinquent);

2. Ask the state franchise tax board to withhold your tax return;

3. Contract with an outside collection agency to handle it;****

4. Request that the federal government get involved in the collection (assuming it's a federal loan). The federal government may either assist the college, or the college could return it to the government and let them worry about it.

---

* There is a loan origination fee of 5% on Guaranteed Student Loans. The lender takes the fee out of the amount of the loan, but you are required to pay back the full amount of the loan (including the 5% you never received). There is also a 1% insurance premium fee deducted from the loan.

** If you borrowed money under the old 7% interest rate (prior to 1981) you have a nine-month grace period on its repayment.

***Loans made before 1981 have a 7% interest rate; loans made between 1981 and October 1983 have a 9% rate. Loans made after October 1983 are at 8%.

****The American National Educational Corp. in Chicago handles student loan default accounts for over 450 colleges in the country, including the University of California.

As we discuss in more detail in Section F, if any of the first three options are taken, the applicable statute of limitations will be four years (in California). If the federal government gets involved, a six-year statute applies and only begins from the time the feds pay off the original lender.

C. How to Handle Bank or College Loans

Generally, the way to deal with these bank or college loans is pretty much the same as the handling of any other debts. See Chapter 7 on collection agencies. But here are a few things to consider.

Your bargaining power with banks will probably be more limited than with colleges. Bank loans require a $30 a month minimum repayment plan. If you cannot afford that amount, you might try to work something else out, but probably it won't work. The bank would just as well turn the loan over to the government, collect all their money, and not worry about it. However, once the government holds the loan agreement, you probably would be able to work out a more convenient payment schedule. The government or the collection agency, having no one to turn the loan over to, may well accept a reasonable payment schedule in order to avoid having to go through the hassle of filing a lawsuit and trying to collect on the judgment.

With loans from colleges, you usually have much more flexibility than with banks. Though they too will often say they require a $30 minimum repayment, if they do not get it there isn't much they can do (though some will hold back diplomas or transcripts until payments are made). And colleges aren't going to contract out to a collection agency if they can avoid it. After all, you are an alumnus. So, explain your situation and offer them what you can afford. Most likely they will be pleased that you are honestly trying to cooperate. Usually, though, they will ask you to agree to extend the statute of limitations as part of the agreement (see Section F, below).

Here is a sample letter of the type you might send to your college to work out a repayment schedule.

---

612 Pumpkin Road
Riverside, California
March 1, 19___

Donald Juneau
Student Loan Department
Arthur Rackham University
Alexandria Street
Big Sur, California

Dear Mr. Juneau:

I was graduated from Arthur Rackham University in June, 19___. While at the school, I borrowed $3,000 in National Direct Student Loans. I realize that my 9-month grace period is nearly over and that I must begin making payments soon.

In your letter of February 3, you said that I must repay a minimum of $30 per month. However, I have recently taken a job as a fortune teller for Hometown Mystics and my income barely covers my expenses. Nevertheless, I realize my obligations to repay and I do not want to back out from these obligations.

Consequently, I wish to make payments of $15 a month at this time. Should I get a raise later on, I will try to increase my payments.

Very truly yours,

Christopher Michael Campbell

D. Filing Bankruptcy

You must now wait five years from the time the loan is first due (usually nine months after you leave school) before you can discharge it in bankruptcy. The only exception is if you can prove that it would be "undue hardship" to you or your family if the loan is not included in your bankruptcy petition. There is no clear definition of what exactly qualifies as undue hardship, though it means something more than ordinary difficulties. Generally, you must say you are the victim of accident or illness and you have minimized all personal expenditures and exhausted all efforts to find employment. You might want to speak to a lawyer if you are thinking of filing under this provision [11 U.S.C. Section 523(a)(8)]. In some California cities, by using the wage earner plan (Chapter 13) you may be able, in effect, to get rid of your loan without having to wait five years. It depends on how much the bankruptcy court in your area decides you need to pay to show "good faith" in trying to deal with your debts under a Chapter 13 repayment plan (see Chapter 18, Section N).

NOTE: Many student loans require co-signers. If the original debtor (the student) goes bankrupt, the lender can still go after the co-signer. This can also be done if the debtor simply refuses to pay (see Chapter 1 on co-signers).

E. Federal Government Reprisals

The government has become more aggressive and will try to apply sanctions if you default on their loans. Some agencies say that they will deny you federal assistance later on because of your "bad record." We have heard, for example that the Housing and Urban Development Office says they may not approve certain guaranteed housing loans if you have not repaid your school debts. It is even possible that filing bankruptcy on the loan can cause prob-

lems on future government loan applications. The Federal Government has also begun to give private credit bureaus the names of students who do not pay back these loans. And, unless you can convince the Federal Government that a mistake was made (or that the loan is legally unenforceable), that fat tax refund you were expecting may evaporate into thin air.

F. Statute of Limitations

If the U.S. government sues to collect on the loan, the statute of limitations is six years. This means the suit must be filed within six years of when your debt legally became collectable by the federal government.

If the lender or a collection agency sues you, the statute of limitations is the length of time provided in your state's laws for bringing suit on a written contract (the state in which you obtained the loan). In California, this period is four years from when the debt legally became delinquent (i.e., when you missed your payment).

About the only defense normally available in court actions for the collection of delinquent student loans is that this statute of limitations period has elapsed. Because of the sheer quantity of student loans, and the likewise unwieldy numbers of defaulting ex-students, there are often lengthy delays between the time you fail to meet your installment schedule and the time anybody does something about it. A lot can happen in that time.

Suppose one day a notice comes out of the blue, "Dear Mr. Jones, we have not received a payment on your student loan since January 1977 [it's now August 1987] and would appreciate your contacting us at your earliest convenience.

Sincerely, ... " Suppose you say to yourself, "I really need every penny right now and can't afford to pay the [federal government, college, collection agency, or whomever] anything." If this sounds familiar, the statute of limitations is probably the most promising avenue to explore.

Because most student loans are guaranteed by the federal government, we will first show how the statute of limitations operates when the feds try to collect their loan in court. After that, we'll explore a few details to watch for when the lender or collection agency files the suit.

1. Federally-Insured Loans

As we mentioned, if your loan is "turned back" to the federal government under the guaranteed student loan program, and the feds sue you to collect (or propose a deduction from your tax refund), the statute of limitations is six years. However, this time period only begins to run when the federal government pays off the lender, which must be done within 90 days after they receive the loan back from the lender.*

EXAMPLE A: Assume Tom obtained a loan from the Bank of El Cerrito through one of the federal student loan programs. He defaulted on his payments and first the bank sent him a couple of warning letters and then turned the loan over to the federal government on January 5, 1980. The federal government paid the bank off on April 4, 1980 (within the 90-day period) and then contracted the loan out for collection. The collection agency sent a couple of threatening letters to Tom and then laid off for awhile. Finally, in January 1986, seven years after he was supposed to start making payments on the loan, Tom gets sued, with the U.S. Government listed as plaintiff.

---

* U.S. V. FRISK, 675 F.2d 1079 (9th Cir (1982); U.S. V. WILSON, 478 F.Supp. 488 (N.D. PA 1979).

Since the action is being "brought" by the federal government, the statute of limitations is six years, and only began to run from the time the feds paid back the lender, or April 1980. Since the suit was filed less than six years after that date, there is no valid statute of limitations defense. (The time elapsed between April 1980 and January 1986 is five years and nine months.)

EXAMPLE B: Assume that Tom obtained a loan through his college and when he defaulted on the payments either the college tried to collect it on its own, or sold the loan to a collection agency which initiated the collection efforts. If the loan is not referred back to the federal government, and was obtained in California, the applicable statute of limitations is four years, whether the loan was through the Guaranteed Student Loan Program, the National Defense Student Loan program, or some local program.

2. Waivers of the Statute of Limitations

If you waived the statute in your original loan agreement and the loan was turned back to the federal government for collection, you may have no statute of limitations defense.

If you waived the statute of limitations as a condition of extending your time to make payments or lessening them, you will have re-established the applicable statute of limitations period. If you then subsequently fail to pay in such a situation, the statute will start all over again.

If you either make a partial payment, or give notice of your intent to start paying, the statute of limitations will start running anew for the entire loan from the time such payments are made. In other words, by making or offering to make any payments, you retrigger the six-year statute of limitations from that time forward.

NOTE: This is unlike the normal situation in California, where the partial payment of a debt does not affect the statute of limitations as to the balance (this may differ in other states).

EXAMPLE A: Janice borrowed money from the Guaranteed Student Loan Program in 1979. She became a half-time student in 1980 and graduated in January 1981. She made no payments. In November 1981, the bank turned the loan over to the federal government, which paid it off in December 1981. No payments were made for the following four years. In 1986, a collection agency contacted Janice, who now had a good job. She agreed to pay $50.00 per month. The effect of this is to start the six-year federal limitations period running again, which means that even if Janice didn't make the payment, she could be sued for collection by the government until 1992.

EXAMPLE B: The facts are the same as above, except that Janice made no agreement, but simply sent in $50.00 in 1986. The statute would still start running again from that payment until 1992.

EXAMPLE C: Again, the facts are the same as in Example A, but this time Janice agrees in 1986 to waive the statute of limitations in exchange for the government accepting lower payments. Such agreement would at least start the statute running again as in the other examples and quite possibly would eliminate the defense forever.

3. Loans Not Turned over to the Federal Government

As we mentioned, some loans are not insured by the federal government but rather arranged through the college or bank directly. Also, in some cases, a federally-insured loan may not be turned back to the federal government for collection but rather handled locally by the lender or a collection agency.

When you are sued on a loan with anyone other than the federal government as plaintiff, you will be dealing with the statute of limitations of the state in which you obtained the loan. These will differ from state to state, and we are only going to get specific in regard to the California statute of limitations for suits on written contracts. Thus, if you obtained your loan in another state, you'll need to go to a law library and find the relevant statute of limitations for written contracts for that state. When you do your research about the laws of the state where you obtained your loan, make sure you pay attention to how the concepts discussed in this chapter are handled in that state. The operative jargon is 1) statute of limitations for written contracts; 2) installment payments; 3) acceleration clause; 4) waiver of the statute of limitations; and 5) "tolling of the statute of limitations." See Chapter 3.

For you to understand how the California statute of limitations for written contracts applies to student loans, we first need to introduce the following several concepts. You'll see how they come into play later in the discussion:

■ Almost all student loan contracts involve installment payments beginning after you leave school;

■ Almost all student loan contracts have a provision called an "acceleration clause" which entitles the bank, college, collection agency, etc. to require that the entire loan be paid back immediately if you have defaulted on your payments.

■ Statutes of limitations can be suspended or "tolled" for the period of time during which you don't have to pay, such as when you re-enroll in school, or when you leave the jurisdiction (the state or country). More about this later.

Now, let's discuss the California statute of limitations as it relates to student loans not turned over to the federal government for collection. There are several variables which may have a profound effect on how the statute of limitations will be applied to your case.

a. Installment Payments

If your loan contract involves installment payments, then the statute of limitations begins to run when the first installment is missed <u>as to that installment only</u>. Assume, for example, that the applicable statute is four years, as it is on loans obtained in California which are not turned back to the federal government for collection. Assume further that your payback period is ten years.

The statute will not totally protect you from having to repay every installment until 14 years after your first installment became due, unless the loan was accelerated (discussed directly following this point). However, the statute will protect you in regard to the particular installments which were missed in four years. In other words, so long as four years or more separate a court action against you from a particular missed installment payment, the court action is not allowed <u>as to that installment</u>.

EXAMPLE: Tom borrowed $6,000 during his school years. He was expected to pay off the loan in $50 monthly payments beginning six months after he left school, which was in June 1979. His first payment did not fall due until January 1, 1980. He never made a payment.

If the applicable statute of limitations is four years, on January 2, 1984 the statute would have run, <u>but only in regard to the one installment</u>, which was originally due on January 1, 1980. On February 2, 1984 the statute of limitations would have run, but only in regard to the February 1980 payment. Because Tom's payback period is ten years ($50 x 12 = $600 x 10 = $6,000), it would take the full ten years plus the four-year limitations period before Tom would be totally absolved of liability as to all installments.

b. Acceleration of the Loan

If the owner of the loan notifies you that the full amount is due and payable because of your default (i.e., if they invoke the acceleration clause), then the statute of limitations as to <u>all</u> remaining installments begins to run from that time.

EXAMPLE: Assume that in Tom's case, the college which loaned him the money sent him a letter in January 1984, reminding him that he was several years behind on his payments, and that since he had not contacted them or responded to their letters, the entire amount of the loan was being accelerated and that the $6,000 was therefore due and payable now.

In this case, Tom would be working on two statutes of limitations periods. The first period would involve the several years worth of installment payments which he missed. The second period, triggered by the acceleration of the debt would begin running as to the rest of the loan. Thus, if no suit were brought within four years after the acceleration letter (assuming we're dealing with the California statute), Tom would be off the hook for the entire loan.

c. Waiver of the California Statute of Limitations

If you signed a "waiver" of the statute of limitations in order to get your loan, and it was obtained in California and has not been turned back to the federal government, the law provides that an additional four years is tacked on as a result of your waiver. This means that the statute would be eight years instead of four.

However, if you only made a partial payment, or orally offered to pay in the future, such actions do not affect the operation of the statute of limitations in California.

d. Suspending the "Running of" The Statute

The statute of limitations is suspended ("tolled" in legal jargon) for all loans for any period that you are back in school half-time or more. If a loan not turned over to the federal government is involved, the statute of limitations is also suspended for any period when you were out-of-state where you obtained the loan.

This is a very tricky area. When a statute of limitations starts to operate in respect to a debt (i.e., when the debt becomes delinquent), it is said to start "running." Under ordinary circumstances, the statute continues "running" until the period elapses, or a court action is filed, whichever occurs first.

Under certain circumstances, such as the ones mentioned above, the statute "stops running" as a matter of law. In that case, the statute is "tolled" for such time as it has stopped running. Let's look at two examples.

EXAMPLE A: Kathleen obtained a student loan in California while at college and graduated in June 1975. Her first payments became due in January 1976. She didn't make them. In June 1976, she enrolled half-time in a special Master's program in a California performing arts school and carried that status for the following two years. She got her master's and promptly moved to New York, where she lived for the next five years. She returned to California in June 1983.

In January 1984 she was served with a court summons on her delinquent student loan (which was not turned back to the federal government and therefore would ordinarily be subject to the four-year California statute). Does she have a statute of limitations defense? No. Why? Between her time in school (two years) and her time out of state (five years), only one year of the four statute "ran" in all that time. The rest of the time the statute was "tolled". If Kathleen was sued on a loan turned back to the federal government, the six-year statute of limitations would be suspended only for the time she was in school, not the time she was out of state, but not in school.

e. How to Use This Information

We've given you a lot of technical information here. Questions about the statute of limitations can be just plain nasty. Whether you are representing yourself or being represented by an attorney in a collection action, we recommend that you have a specific consultation with an attorney about your conclusions regarding the statute of limitations in your case.

Before you do, you should give it your best shot so that when you do talk with the attorney, you'll know the right questions to ask and points to raise. From the information we've provided you, there are clearly several important facts which you should determine beforehand:

■ Did you waive the statute in your original loan contract or in an extension agreement?

■ Was the loan turned back to the federal government? If it was, you'll be sued by the government as plaintiff, even if the suit is conducted by a private lawyer or a collection agency.

■ Were you out of state or in school during the time in question?

■ When did you make installment payments if any?

■ Did you receive any correspondence which could be interpreted as an "acceleration of your loan"?

chapter 16

$ $ $ $ $ $ $

Income Taxes

In a world filled with more and more bureaucrats shuffling more and more pieces of paper saying less and less, there is a tax on everything except the air we breathe. If the air wasn't so filthy, there would probably be a tax on it too. We don't have the ten lifetimes and hundred thousand or so pages necessary to discuss all the problems you can meet by failing to pay all these taxes. Here we limit ourselves to failure to pay state and federal income taxes.

A. Failure to Pay Income Taxes

If you file your tax return, but fail to pay all the money owed, you will get a notice (of assessment) telling you to pay up pronto. This notice establishes a lien against your property (including community property) which lasts for six years. It's a good idea to pay up if possible. The final notice will tell you to pay up immediately or have your wages or property taken. "Immediately" normally means 10 days, although if the IRS determines that collection of the tax is in jeopardy, it may begin collection effort with no delay. The final notice will usually arrive approximately three months after the first notice from the federal tax people and six months after

the first notice from the state. You can sometimes slow down this process by responding in writing to each notice. The notices are sent by a computer. When you respond, someone must get your file and deal with the response. This takes time--sometimes a lot of time. It makes little difference what you say in your letters as long as you don't make any false statements. One good approach is to simply ask for more time to pay and tell the government how hard your life is.

IMPORTANT: If you have been late on your tax payments in the past or have previously failed to pay taxes, you are probably labeled as a "Habitual Delinquent." If this happens, all pretense of politeness is dropped and you will receive only one notice to pay in 10 days or face wage attachments or the loss of other property.

B. Failure to File a Tax Return

If you have paid taxes in the past and suddenly fail to file a return, you will probably be contacted. Should it be determined that you owe money, you will receive a series of notices, as explained in Section A above.

C. Tax Audits

If after a tax audit the government claims you owe more in taxes than you paid, you have the right to several appeals to higher level tax review boards and eventually to Tax Court. As long as you follow up your appeals, which may take several years, no one will get heavy. However, if you fail to appeal in the time allowed, you will receive a series of notices to pay up as outlined in Section A and will face wage attachments and loss of property if you don't. Audits are very tricky. See an attorney or tax accountant before getting involved in one. For an excellent general overview of your right to fight back against what you consider to be improper taxation by either the Federal or California Government, see TAX PRACTICE IN CALIFORNIA, Continuing Education of the Bar, available in any California law library.

D. Tax Collections

The federal tax collector does not have to go to court to get a judgment against you before taking your wages and property.* None of the exemptions discussed in Chapters 10, 11 and 12 work against federal tax claims. However, IRC Section 6334 exempts the following property from federal tax levy without court action: (1) wearing apparel and school books: (2) fuel, provisions, furniture, and personal effects not more than $1500 in value; (3) books and tools of a trade, business or profession, not more than $1000 in value; (4) unemployment benefits; (5) undelivered mail; (6) certain annuity and pension payments, and workers' compensation; (8) as much of income as is needed to make support payments for minor children, as ordered by a court before the levy; (9) minimum

amount of wages or salary for personal services, or other income.

The State of California tax collector similarly does not have to spend time suing you and getting a judgment. However, the state has decided to recognize a debtor's right to the exemptions discussed earlier. If you owe state tax and the government goes after your wages, personal property or dwelling house, you may file for a Claim of Exemption to protect the item, just as you would if a regular creditor were trying to attach it. If the state goes after your wages without a court hearing, it can take up to 25% of your net earnings. If this happens, you may request an administrative hearing to reconsider or modify the amount to be withheld. If the state files an application in court to attach your wages, it can take a much larger portion--up to 50%.**

The amount will depend upon what portion of your earnings you can prove is necessary for the support of yourself and/or your family.

Wage earners who have little in the way of valuable belongings can usually work out some form of monthly payments to catch up on unpaid taxes to the federal government, but the payments will be quite high. The government does not have to make this sort of arrangement, but it often will because if it takes your whole paycheck, you are likely to quit your job in disgust.

---

* Internal Revenue Code Section 63.31 "includes the power of distraint and seizure by any means."

** Cal. Civil Code Sections 2983.2 and 2983.3 or Financial Code Sections 22465 and 24465, depending on who the creditor is.

chapter 17

$ $ $ $ $ $ $

Child Support and Spousal Support (Alimony)

Someplace over the dream rainbow of a man, a woman and their children living a happy, loving, harmonious life in which fulfillment is either complete, or just around the next split-level ranch house, lies reality. Marriage just isn't working for lots of people--hundreds of thousands are involved in divorce proceedings every year. Divorce creates lots of money problems for lots of people, especially children. They like to eat, live in comfortable places, and have an occasional lollipop. Divorce often puts these things in jeopardy. For those with low or moderate incomes, there is simply not enough money to support two households. An impossible situation is created in which something has to give.

A. Child Support — The Holy Obligation

Before we take a detailed look at the child support obligation from the standpoint of the person who owes it, there is one overriding point which we need to make at the outset. Simply put, people who owe child support who have any income at all can't win. In large part, this is because legislatures and courts have decided that the solution to the societal problem of poverty in single parent families is to wring increased amounts of support out of the absent or non-custodial parent (almost always the father). Accordingly, the devices available for enforcement of child support obligations have multiplied like rabbits, at the same time they have become as strong as grizzly bears.

In the face of these developments, our advice to those of you who have child support obligations is: Continue to meet your child support obligation or, where appropriate, promptly seek a court modification of your obligation to an amount which you can afford. Fortunately, California has a simplified do-it-yourself procedure permitting a decrease in child support when there is a sudden decrease in income. All the forms and guidance you need to obtain a modification can be found in THE CHILD SUPPORT AND CUSTODY HANDBOOK, Matthews, Siegel and Willis (Nolo Press). We provide a brief overview of the how the procedure works in Section D of this chapter.

Whatever you do, don't stick your head in the sand hoping the bad news that you owe more child support than you can pay will pass. It won't.

B. Child Support as Part of a Divorce Case

As part of a divorce proceeding, there is always an order for child support if there are children younger than 18. Either party can be ordered to support the children, but even though sex roles are changing rapidly, it is still usually the man. It is wise to pay child support on time and in full.*

If the parent ordered to support willfully fails to do so, he is in what is known as "contempt of court." Translated, this means "big trouble." After a court hearing, he can be sent to county jail. In legal jargon the "contempt citation" process is called an "Order to Show Cause." This is an order to show up in court at a certain date and time to explain why you have not paid. A person receiving an "Order to Show Cause" concerning contempt better show up and better have a good story. Those who fail to attend will quickly be picked up on a warrant, tossed in jail for a day or two, and escorted in to see the judge in handcuffs. Those who show up voluntarily but don't have a good story may enter the courthouse by the front door, but will certainly leave in a paddy wagon for a few days of free education behind county walls.

Of course, in addition to the criminal and civil contempt procedures outlined

in this chapter, child support can be collected by all the normal methods of collecting judgments--wage, bank account, and personal property attachments, liens against real estate, etc.

Wages can be assigned up to 50% for child support (and spousal support) debts. The procedure goes as follows: If the parent who is responsible for child support payments (let's call the parent the "father") fails to make the equivalent of one month's payment within a 24-month period, the parent to whom support has been ordered (the "mother") can sign an affidavit and petition the court to assign the wages of the father to satisfy the child support payment(s). Thus, the missing of one monthly payment or only paying half of two month's support obligations would both satisfy the statute. However, the mother must first notify the father 15 days before she files this petition that she intends to seek this court relief of wage assignment. The court issues, without notice to the father, an order of assignment of wages to satisfy the court-ordered support.** There is a 10-day period after the father's employer has been served before he must deliver to the father a copy of the assignment order.

If the father contends that his failure to pay did not occur within the last 24 months, or that he owes nothing, he can move to "quash" the assignment order, but he must do so within 10 days after service by his employer. In the meantime, the father's employer must continue to withhold and forward support as ordered by the court until he is notified that the court has granted the father's motion. The law also specifically provides that no employer shall use any assignment of wages as grounds for dismissal of the father. (Civil Code Section 4701.)

An order assigning salary or wages takes precedence over any assignment to other creditors. The court will order the employer to withhold and assign the regular child support payments of a certain sum per month until the arrearage is paid off. Combined, these amounts

---

* Child support and custody as well as community and separate property and other legal rules affecting the marriage are discussed in CALIFORNIA MARRIAGE & DIVORCE LAW, Warner and Ihara, Nolo Press (see back of this book).

** This order stays in effect until all payments are current. If a second petition is granted within 24 months, it automatically lasts for 24 months. If a third petition is granted in 48 months, it is perpetual.

cannot exceed 50% of the father's income.

If the District Attorney is involved in collecting this support from you, he may agree to accept less money. Therefore it is important that you pay attention to any court summons and show up at a hearing.

Important: The existence of many other debts is absolutely no excuse not to pay child support. Similarly, the fact that a person spends money to support someone else's kids is not a legal excuse not to support his own. There are tens of thousands of Californians who each year fail to take their support obligations seriously. It is one reason why county jails are so overcrowded.

If a couple can agree to a child support amount as part of a compatible divorce, fine. If they can't and the matter goes into court contested, it is wise to have an attorney (see Chapter 3). Child support is always changeable as circumstances change. Either party can petition the court to either raise or lower the amount at any time.*

If you are in agreement, it is relatively easy to make this sort of change yourself, by using the forms and instructions for child support modification proceedings contained in THE CHILD CUSTODY AND SUPPORT HANDBOOK, by Matthews, Siegel, and Willis, Nolo Press (see back of this book for order information).

Even if you are not in agreement, California has established a do-it-yourself procedure which (1) permits child support modifications of up to 10% of the overall obligation for each year which has passed since child support was last set, and 2) permits modifications of any amount when there has been a sudden decrease in income. For instance, suppose in January 1984 Jerry was ordered to pay $200 a month child support. If Jerry's ex-spouse desired an increase in support in January 1987, she could obtain a 30% increase in support (10% for each of the three years since the current amount was set). And (theoretically) Jerry could use this same procedure to obtain a 30% decrease. Further,

---
* Easy do-it-yourself forms available to increase support 10% per year. No court hearing is necessary unless there is an objection. See Matthews, Siegel & Willis, *The Child Custody and Support Handbook* (Nolo Press) for complete "how to" instructions.

if Jerry lost his job, he might obtain a larger decrease if his income and expense statement submitted to the court warranted it.

Generally, this simplified procedure may only be used once a year. However, the statute makes an exception to this rule for modifications which are based on a sudden decrease in income. Continuing our example, if after obtaining a 30% decrease in July of 1986 Jerry suffers a sudden decline in income (e.g., due to job loss or lay-off), he may go back to court for another reduction under this simple proceeding.

How does this simple procedure work? The person seeking a modification fills out a form requesting the change, a form containing the proposed order, and a form showing the person's income and expenses. These filled-in forms are then filed with the court and copies are served on the other parent.

If the other parent desires to contest the request, he or she must file a response and request a hearing. If there is no contest, the court may then grant all or part of the modification without a hearing. However, if the request for a decreased support obligation is based on a sudden decrease in income, the court will want clear evidence of this in the requestor's income and expense statements.

This entire process is designed to work without an attorney. In fact, attorneys may not appear at the hearing in the event one is scheduled. However, if the responding parent desires to be represented, and files a statement to this effect, the proceedings are no longer conducted under the simplified modification statute. Instead, they are handled like a regular modification motion.

Complete forms and instructions for initiating and responding to a simplified modification can be found in THE CHILD CUSTODY AND SUPPORT HANDBOOK, Matthews, Siegel and Willis, Nolo Press.

Important: Shortly after this new simplified support system went into effect, the California legislature passed the Agnos Child Support Standards Act of 1984 (discussed in Section E below and in much more detail in THE CHILD CUSTODY AND SUPPORT HANDBOOK. The

Agnos Act is in some respects inconsistent with the simplified procedure. For instance, under the simplified procedure a judge is authorized to grant a modification without seeing an income and expense statement, whereas the Agnos Act requires such forms to be submitted in all proceedings affecting child support. Also, despite the 10% per year modification permitted under the simplified procedure, the Agnos Act requires child support to be set no lower than certain minimums established in the Act, and higher if the parties can afford it. Simply put, it may not be as easy to obtain these modifications as it was prior to the Agnos Act taking effect.

Important: Child support obligations are not dischargeable in bankruptcy. Also, certain attorney fees of the person receiving child support can't be wiped out in bankruptcy. This is a tricky area of the law and it is wise to consult a lawyer.

C. Failure to Support Your Child Is a Crime

The California legislature has done everything in its power to insure that children are supported. Penal Code Section 270 states that the willful failure of a parent to support his or her children is a crime punishable by a fine of up to $1,000 and a jail sentence of up to one year, or both. It makes no difference whether the child's parents were married, or whether or not there has been a divorce proceeding.* If a father is disabled and has no income or savings, failure to support is not a crime. If he is unemployed, he will not be prosecuted as long as he can show he is diligently seeking work. A court, in determining the ability of a father to support, will consider all of his income, including social insurance and gifts. If a father dies, or is otherwise unable to support, the duty falls on the mother.

When county authorities learn that a father is not supporting, they assign an employee of the District Attorney's Office, Family Support Division, to the case in situations where the mother is on welfare or may be forced to apply for welfare if support is not received.** Where welfare benefits are involved, an eligibility worker will alert the District Attorney automatically. The D.A.'s office first requests that the non-supporting father come in for a conference. It is an excellent idea to attend this sort of conference. Those who fail to do so are very likely to have a formal criminal action for failure to support initiated against them. The purpose of the conference is to establish how much the father earns, whether or not he has other children to support, and to arrange for him to start making support payments. Be prepared to be shocked by how much the D.A. wants. Children are expensive, and the Family Support Division normally tries to collect as much as the traffic will bear. By pointing out other obligations and the necessity of going to the grocery store now and then, a father can often get the county to agree to payments slightly less than those first proposed.

Once an amount has been agreed upon, it is important to make payments promptly and in full unless there is a good reason, such as illness or loss of work, to do otherwise. If there is such a reason it is important that the Family Support Division be told immediately what the problems are.

Note: California and the U.S. Government now cooperate so that individuals who owe past-due child support which has been assigned to the state for collection (through local District Attorney's offices) can have their income tax refunds withheld. This is done through use of social security numbers and may involve the parent locator service if a parent's whereabouts are not known. So, if you have been sued by a District Attorney for back child support or your wages have been assigned for collection under Civil Code Section 4701 and you still owe child support arrearage, you can expect to have your income tax refund used to pay your support. See Section 42 U.S.C. Section 664 for more information.

---

* The rights and obligations of unmarried couples are discussed in detail in *The Living Together Kit,* Ihara and Warner, Nolo Press (see back of this book).

** If the father can't be located, the county can get access to federal social security information to find him. Once found, prosecution is simply transferred to the county where the father resides.

Important: What happens if a District Attorney seeks a higher amount of support than has been ordered by the court in a dissolution or modification proceeding? Two California courts of appeal have split on this issue. The court of appeal for the Los Angeles area has held that the District Attorney is stuck with the amount ordered by the court in the dissolution or modification action. Conversely, the court of appeal for the San Jose area* has ruled that the District Attorney is entitled to seek and obtain a higher amount. In all likelihood, this issue will ultimately be decided by the California Supreme Court. To some extent, this issue will not be as important as it once was, due to the new requirement that all child support obligations be assessed according to statewide standards set by the Agnos Act (covered in the next section).

A divorce order, if there is one, takes priority over any agreement made with the District Attorney's Office. This means that county authorities will not bother a person who is in compliance with the child support provisions of a divorce order. It also means, however, that if a divorce order is entered setting child support at an amount higher than requested by the District Attorney, you must pay this higher amount.** It is perfectly possible to be hauled into court for civil contempt for failing to pay the full child support amount set out in a divorce order (see Part A of this chapter), even though you are diligently paying a lower amount requested by the District Attorney.

D. New Child Support Minimums

On July 1, 1985, the rules for setting child support amounts changed radically. Convinced that child support awards should be more uniform and less subject to local variation, the California legislature imposed a uniform standard on

the courts for determining child support levels. Here is a simple outline of how the new law works. For detailed guidance in computing child support obligations and seeking modifications under the new act (called the Agnos Child Support Standards Act of 1984), consult THE CHILD CUSTODY AND SUPPORT HANDBOOK, by Matthews, Siegel and Willis (Nolo Press).

The basic purpose of the Agnos Act is to impose child support obligations on both parents that will, at a minimum, assure the child the same level of support as his benefits would be under the Aid to Families With Dependent Children welfare program. Also, to the extent that parents can afford a larger amount of support, the courts are encouraged to order it.

The first step to computing these obligations is to use a court form for determining the income available to each parent for the payment of such support (termed the parent's "annual net disposable income").

After each parent's annual net disposable income is toted up, the joint result is multiplied by 18% for one child, 27% for two children, 36% for three children, 40% for four children, 44% for five children, and an additional 4% for each additional child up to ten children. If the result is less than the AFDC standard for that number of children, the child support shall be set at the lower amount. If the result is greater than the AFDC standards, then the minimum will be set at the AFDC level.

Once the overall support obligation to the children is computed, the next step is to figure out what each parent's obligation will be. This depends on the proportion of the total income that each parent's separate income represents. For instance, if one parent's income is two-thirds of the total while the other parent's income is one-third, their respective obligations would be equal to these proportions.

Once the parent's respective obligation is computed, it is next necessary to decide who actually has to part with the cash. In situations where one parent has sole physical custody, this

---

* County of Santa Clara v. Farnese, 173 Cal.App. 3d.60 (1985).

** If a parent falls one month behind in paying child support and the matter is brought to court, a judge will automatically order that his or her wages be assigned. Civil Code Section 4701.

determination is easy--the non-custodial parent pays the custodial parent. In the event parents share joint physical custody, however, the amount is worked out under different principles.

The Agnos law permits divorcing parents who have not applied for public assistance or assigned their support rights to the county to agree to a support arrangement that provides less support than the mandatory minimum. However, the courts are instructed not to improve such agreements unless the parties are aware of the mandatory minimums and state that their children will be adequately supported by them.

This entire discussion so far has focused on the minimum child support standards that must be satisfied in both original dissolutions and modification proceedings. However, the law is not satisfied with children only receiving the minimum. Under the Agnos Act, courts are required to consider whether parents can afford to pay a higher amount of support.

In deciding whether an additional amount is warranted, the courts will be considering county-recommended support schedules prepared especially for this purpose. To the extent that a county has not adopted such a schedule by July 1986, the courts in that county will have to follow a supplementary state schedule due to be published by that date (Civil Code Section 4724).

Low income parents who have negotiated payment amounts with a district attorney's office can expect to have these raised, although not necessarily to one-third of their disposable income, as required by Sections 4720-4727. This is true even though the D.A. operates under criminal law standards which basically hold that no one can be jailed or fined for failure to pay child support unless they have the ability to do so. In other words, if you can only possibly afford $50 per month per child because you have a very low income, the D.A. can't succeed in a criminal prosecution against you for not paying more. However--and this is the important part-- because the legislature has significantly raised the minimum they consider to be acceptable, you can be sure that the District Attorney's offices will demand more too.

E. Spousal Support (Alimony)

Spousal support (alimony), a necessary fact of life a generation ago, is for the most part outdated today. The woman who 20 years ago gave up school and other opportunities to devote herself to husband and children often needed support when the marriage went sour. Many times she was educationally and psychologically unable to support herself. Today this is far less true, but spousal support still exists.

Spousal support, in theory, can be awarded to either men or women. In fact, it is almost always given to women. Judges, being old, and often from upper middle class backgrounds, still tend to think the world is like it was when they were in law school and all people of their social class received spousal support. A 65-year-old judge has a lot of trouble relating to the life realities of people 30 to 40 years younger (mostly the people who get divorces). The result is that judges grant spousal support more often than is necessary.

The subject of spousal support comes up automatically as part of a divorce. Most younger women don't want it, desiring child support if they have children, but not wanting support for themselves. Older women want, and need, spousal support more often. Of course, a housewife of fifty who has raised a family and helped her husband become financially successful is entitled to a generous support award.

Failure to pay spousal support is not a crime. However, one can be found in contempt of court for willfully failing to pay spousal support if one has the ability to do so. As we said above, when discussing child support, a person can be sent to county jail for this sort of "contempt." A person's wages, bank account, personal property and tax refund can be attached if spousal support is not paid. Also, the spouse owed the support is entitled to any reasonable attorney fees necessary to collect it.

If no spousal support is awarded as part of a divorce proceeding, it can't be awarded later, unless the court specifically orders an exact amount of money for a limited period of time (i.e. $300 per month for four years). If, for example, the court order said "$300 per month until death, remarriage or further order of court," the amount could be changed by the judge at any time upon the petition of either husband or wife. Of course, both parties would get a chance to present their arguments to the judge if a change were proposed. Spousal support automatically ends upon the remarriage of the person receiving it.

Important: Spousal support obligations are not dischargeable in bank-ruptcy. Also, certain attorney fees of the person receiving spousal support can't be wiped out in bankruptcy. Spousal support obligations are generally a tricky area of the law and it is wise to consult a lawyer (see Chapter 3).

We include here guidelines used by judges in Marin County in awarding spousal support. Remember, these are only guidelines and should be changed to fit the facts of each individual situation.

GUIDELINES FOR DURATION OF SPOUSAL SUPPORT AFTER DISSOLUTION OR LEGAL SEPARATION

Length of Marriage

• Under 12 years: It is presumed that spousal support shall terminate after a period equivalent to one-half the duration of the marriage.

• 12 to 25 years: There is no presumption for termination of spousal support. The following factors to be considered (whether or not it shall terminate): wife's education, training, work experience, health and age; husband's ability to pay support; wife's eligibility for social security.

• Over 25 years: It is presumed that permanent spousal support shall not terminate unless wife remarries.

   1. Presence or absence of preschool children to be considered if husband has income above minimum.

   2. Special consideration to be given to the ill health of either spouse.

   3. After 25 years of marriage, the wife is presumed to require spousal support.

   4. Duration of temporary spousal support payments should be taken into account.

AMOUNT OF SPOUSAL SUPPORT

If the net earnings of one spouse are $300.00 to $600.00, maximum support to the other spouse is one-third of that income.

If the net earnings of one spouse are over $600.00, maximum support to the other spouse shall not exceed 40% of that amount.

If there is both spousal and child support, the combined order should not exceed 50% of the supporting spouse's net income.

No spousal support shall be provided to any spouse, who following dissolution, has income sufficient to maintain his or her standard of living.

chapter 18

$ $ $ $ $ $ $

Bankruptcy

Want to get rid of all your debts at one time? Your creditors have been harassing you and you are at your wits end trying to cope. Perhaps your wages have been garnished, or bill collectors have made it clear that a garnishment is just around the corner. As we have indicated throughout this book, you do have one ultimate weapon--bankruptcy. If, after reading this book carefully you feel that bankruptcy is the only sensible course of action, you or your lawyer can quickly eliminate the great majority of your debts by filing some simple papers.*

---

* The best source of further information on bankruptcy is Kosel, BANKRUPTCY: DO IT YOURSELF, Nolo Press (see back of this book for more information).

A. What Is It?

Bankruptcy was set up by the federal government to help you wipe out most, if not all of your debts. Your debts to the butcher, the baker, the candlestick maker, the doctor, the oil company, the finance company, the phone company, and the furniture store can all be eliminated. Very few debts cannot be wiped out with a bankruptcy, and we'll talk about those later on.

You can file bankruptcy at any time. It doesn't matter whether you're working or not. The only restriction is that you must wait six years between filings. Bankruptcy is a relatively simple procedure involving filing some papers in federal court, paying a $60 filing fee, and paying attorney's fees of somewhere between $200 and $500, unless you choose to do it yourself.

If you have any "assets" of value ("assets" are anything you own, including money), the bankruptcy court may take some of these and use them to pay off your creditors. But the law has made a large exception here and permits you to keep part, and often all, of your possessions. You can usually keep an inexpensive car, your home, and tools or equipment you need in your trade or profession. These assets are called "exempt" assets and are explained in Section F below.

Bankruptcy is a powerful remedy. It's as if you took a blanket and laid it over all your debts, recited a few magic words, removed the blanket and poof!--your debts are gone. But like any powerful remedy, it only works well if used with care and understanding. Just as you wouldn't undertake a major operation to remove a wart, you wouldn't file bankruptcy to eliminate a debt of $1,000.

B. Why Feel Guilty?

"Low down-payments," "easy credit," "36 months to pay,"--so goes the salesman's song. You are bombarded with special deals, sales, and every kind of pitch to wear down your resistance and get you to buy and buy and then buy some more. The stores were always so friendly and kind. Then it happened. You missed a payment and suddenly smiles disappeared. They forgot about all the sweet words once sung to you. They wanted the money. And they wanted it immediately. Any way you came up with it was fine. But you had to do it pronto. Soon you got calls at all hours of the day. Letters threatening law suits arrived at your home. "Visitors" from collection agencies came by. Each

time they succeeded in frightening you a bit more. They did their best to make you feel guilty.*

This kind of scare-guilt pattern has been with us for a long time. But so has the concept of bankruptcy, partly as a counteraction to it. In fact, the idea of bankruptcy has been with us for nearly 175 years. Bankruptcy was designed to give people a new start in life at a time when debts are imprisoning them and weighing them down with unnecessary guilt. It exists to give the little guy a chance to get out of the clutches of large corporations. Congress first experimented with a bankruptcy act in 1800. The first modern bankruptcy law was written in 1898 and revised in 1938. This law was entirely re-written in 1978 and took effect in October 1979. Bankruptcy is as American as apple pie, and creditors know it.

Hundreds of those same corporations which entice you into debt and scream the "horrors of bankruptcy" and other terrifying phrases at you use their own good business sense and file bankruptcy each year. So why should you feel any more guilty than they themselves?

C. Are You Getting Divorced?

Often people who are in the process of divorce think of filing bankruptcy. They would like to wipe their whole slate clean and begin again with their new individual lives. But in reality, the financial problems are probably still bound up with the emotional entanglements.

The emotional and financial worries should be kept separate. Remember,

---

* There are several ways to stop this bill collection harassment quickly. See Chapter 7.

except for spousal or child support, you cannot go to jail for not paying your debts. (And even here you can only go to jail if you have the money but refuse to pay. See Chapter 17.) So relax and work out your divorce settlement. Then give thought to your financial problems and figure out the best way to deal with them. You might decide that you need to file bankruptcy to get rid of most debts and be able to pay the important ones-- child and spousal support. Whatever you conclude, at least you'll be on top of it.

D. Debts You Cannot Wipe Out in Bankruptcy

There are certain debts which you must continue to pay even if you file bankruptcy. These are called "non-dischargeable" debts. ("Dischargeable" debts are all the debts you can get rid of in bankruptcy.) Here is a list of the non-dischargeable debts.

1. State and federal taxes

2. Fines (criminal cases, traffic violations, etc.)

3. Child support

4. Spousal support (alimony)*

5. Some lawyers fees connected with a divorce settlement involving support (this is complicated--see an attorney)

6. Claims against you for a willful or malicious act you committed. A willful act is one where you intentionally injure someone or someone's property. These are uncommon. Most automobile accidents, for example, are not intentional but rather the result of negligence, and so are dischargeable in bankruptcy. However, drunk driving resulting in an injury might be considered a willful act.

7. A debt you obtained by fraud or false pretenses, such as by using bad checks or lying on a credit application. A common example of a false financial statement could be where you did not list all the debts you had at the time you were borrowing the money and the creditor relied on the accuracy of your statement in determining whether to lend you the money. If you have any problems here, discuss them with a lawyer before you file.

8. Student loans due for less than five years (see Chapter 15, Section D).

9. Items you purchased recently on credit will not be discharged if the judge determines that you had already decided to file for bankruptcy when you bought them. Judges feel that most people heavily in debt and ready to file for bankruptcy do not go out spending even more--unless they're trying to take advantage of their soon-to-be bankruptcy.

10. Debts you forgot to list on the forms, or which you left off for other reasons (such as thinking you don't really owe them or they'll never go after you for them) are not dischargeable.

---

* A marital property settlement debt which would normally be discharged in bankruptcy is not discharged if, upon examination, the bankruptcy court concludes that it was really intended to be spousal support. SHAVER V. SHAVER (1984) 736 F.2d 1314, 9th Circuit.

11. Credit purchases of $500 or more for luxury goods or services within 40 days of the bankruptcy filing.

12. Loans or cash advances of $1,000 or more within twenty days of the bankruptcy filing.

E. Secured Debts Vs. Unsecured Debts

Secured debts are those in which the creditor keeps legal title of property until you pay off the debt. Unsecured debts are everything else. Most debts you have are probably unsecured (see Chapter 5).

When you file bankruptcy, you wipe out all your unsecured debts. Plus you get to keep any property you bought on that debt. With secured property, however, you must usually give back the merchandise to get rid of the debt.* If you want to keep the item, you must continue making payments on it.

Here is a partial list of unsecured debts:

1. All credit card purchases

2. Utility bills

3. Medical bills

4. Loans from banks, credit unions, and finance companies where no collateral is required--only your signature

5. Union dues

6. Attorney fees

Secured debts would probably be:

---

* However, if you put up exempt household property, such as furniture, as collateral for a loan, and the loan was not made in order for you to purchase the property itself, you can discharge the loan and keep the property. This is discussed in detail in BANKRUPTCY: DO IT YOURSELF, Kosel, Nolo Press.

1. Your car, if you're making payments on it

2. Your house, if you have a mortgage

3. Some furniture, depending on the purchase agreement

4. Other major items such as expensive jewelry, stereo equipment, boats, etc.

If you no longer own the property which is security on a debt because it was lost or stolen or because of some other reason, you may still be responsible for it. If this is your problem, discuss it with your lawyer before you file.

F. Exempt Assets

When you file bankruptcy, you must list all your assets. Your assets are anything you own, including your bank account, personal possessions, and wages. The bankruptcy court may be able to take some of these and use them to pay off your creditors. However, the law has long said that the bankrupt (that is, the person who files bankruptcy) should be able to keep most necessary things. The assets which you can keep are called "exempt" assets and usually include a great deal of what you own.

There are two distinct exemption systems--state and federal. However, under a California law effective January 1, 1985, if you file in California, you must choose one of the two California exemption systems. You cannot select the federal exemption systems. Nor can you select what you think are the best parts of the two California systems. Generally, if you own a home you are probably better off with the California "A" program, since its protection of homes is greater than the California "B" system. If you rent, the California "B" system is likely to be more attractive—it allows for greater flexibility. But only you can decide. Compare the two systems and see.*

CALIFORNIA EXEMPTION SYSTEM "A"

The assets exempt under California exemption system "A" are discussed in detail in Chapters 10, 11, and 12. Go through these and compare them with the California exemption system "B" list below. See which is more favorable to you.

□□□

CALIFORNIA EXEMPTION SYSTEM "B" **

Under this system you can keep:

■ A residence (including a house, housetrailer, mobile home, condominium, houseboat and a burial plot with a total equity up to $7,500).

■ A motor vehicle with an equity of $1,200.

■ Any of the following, as long as your equity in each item is not worth more than $200 (if sold now—not what you paid for it):

- furniture
- appliances
- clothes
- household goods
- books
- animals
- crops
- musical instruments
- health aids

■ Jewelry up to a total equity value of $500;

■ Tools of your trade up to $750 equity;

* A husband and wife must choose the same exemption system.

■ Life insurance, health insurance, disability, retirement benefits, and government benefits such as public assistance, unemployment insurance, veterans' benefits and social security;

■ Awards under a crime victim's reparation law;

■ $7,500 of payments as a result of a bodily injury (not including payments for pain and suffering or lost earnings) and 100 percent of payments in compensation for loss of future earnings.

You also get $400 in any property, plus the unused amount in the first item above. Thus, if you do not own a home, housetrailer, etc., you can take this total of $7,900 ($7,500 + $400) to cover any other property you would like to exempt. These might include bank accounts, a second car, stocks and bonds, or an item which is too expensive to be covered by the exemptions above, e.g., a silver-plated flute valued at more than the $200 exemption for musical instruments.

This $7,900 allowance can give you greater flexibility than can the California exemption "A" system, providing you do not own a home.

EXAMPLE: Shirley, who works as a waitress, owns a car worth $2,000 a harp worth $5,000, and a nine-year-old purebred cocker spaniel named Janice. She also has a checking account with the present balance of $150 and a savings account at a bank with a present balance of $200.

Under California exemption system "A," none of her property is exempt.*** Unless Shirley sells all of her property (before she files for bankruptcy) and closes her bank accounts and puts

** This sytem is actually the old federal exemption system, prior to its revision in 1984.

***However, when the trustee takes her car, Shirley will receive $1,200 in cash—which is the amount of the state exemption for motor vehicles.

the money in exempt assets, she will lose all of it--except her dog, which, with all due respect to Janice, isn't worth enough for the trustee to bother with. But if Shirley picks the California "B" exemption system, she can keep all of her property without bothering about specific exemptions or property transfers, because it is worth less than $7,500.

However, if Shirley owned a home, she might decide to use California exemption system "A". It would protect up to $30,000 of equity in her home, while exemption system "B" would only protect $7,500 of equity.*

G. What About Co-Signers

If someone else, like a friend or family member, signed the loan agreement or contract along with you, then even though you can rid yourself of the debt by filing bankruptcy, unless your cosigner also files, he or she is still responsible for payments. If that other person is, or was, your spouse, you may want him or her to also file bankruptcy with you. Your spouse should probably file if:

1. He or she co-signed the debts;

2. The debts were for necessities

such as rent, food, clothes, and medical bills, and you file for the California exemptions;

3. He or she will be coming into some money, whether by working, inheritance, or whatever. If any terms of the loan agreement or contract were changed during the time it was in effect and the co-signer did not sign accepting the new change, the co-signer may not be responsible for payments. Check with an attorney and see Chapter 1, Section D on co-signers.

H. Business Debts

If you are conducting your own business as a sole proprietor, you may eliminate business debts as part of your bankruptcy with little problem.

If you are conducting your own business as a partnership, you may also list these debts as part of a personal bankruptcy. However, before you do so, you should consult an attorney to discuss the impact of your bankruptcy filing on you, your business, and (most of all)

your partners.

If you are conducting your own business as a corporation, either you or your corporation or both may file for bankruptcy. The choice can be a complicated one. Consult an attorney before deciding.

I. Right Time to File Bankruptcy

The best time to file bankruptcy is when:

■ You are actually going to lose something if you do not file;

■ You do not expect any debts to come up in the near future;

---

* If Shirley were married or the head of a household, her homestead protection would be $45,000. If she were over 65 or physically or mentally disabled and unable to work, her homestead protection would be $55,000. See Chapter 12.

■ You will be able to balance your income and expenses after bankruptcy; and

■ You will actually wipe out debts totaling at least one-third of your yearly income, or one-fourth, if you have a low income.

The following sections will help you figure out when the time is right. Remember, you must wait six years before you can file again. So take the bath fully prepared, and walk away clean. Ask yourself the following:

1. Am I Really Going To Lose Something If I Don't File Now?

If you have a low income and you don't own very much, you may be "judgment proof." Judgment proof means that you have nothing which a creditor can take from you. Filing bankruptcy would be silly, of course, if the creditor can't get anything anyway.

However, if you expect to come into some money soon (other than welfare, social security, unemployment compensation, or other government benefits), perhaps by working or getting an inheritance, you may want to file now. If you don't, the money you receive may be attached by the creditors for payments. By filing bankruptcy, you'll protect yourself by getting rid of these debts for good.

2. Do I Expect Any Debts To Come Up In The Near Future?

If you expect to be owing more money in the near future, such as for hospital or medical bills, or because of an accident where you were at fault and didn't have insurance, be sure these are also included.

3. Will I Be Able To Balance My Income And Expenses After Bankruptcy?

People are often so anxious to file bankruptcy to solve all their problems that they never think of what their financial situation will be afterwards. Yet, if it is no better than before, you will have wasted your opportunity to file.

Give a little thought to what your financial position will be after you wipe out your present debts. Will you soon be accumulating new debts, or will you be able to keep your new financial position in harmony with the life style you want to live?

Take a look at the chart below. Fill it out and see where it leads you. If it leads you nowhere, bankruptcy may not do you much good.

FINANCIAL POSITION AFTER BANKRUPTCY

Monthly Expenses

Rent or Mortgage Payments and
Utilities
Food
Medical Bills
Clothes
Property Taxes
Alimony or Child Support
Transportation
Entertainment
Other Expenses

TOTAL

Monthly Income

    Employment
    Other Source of Income
    Food Stamps

    _____
    _____
    _____
    _____

    TOTAL

========================

Now look at these totals. Unless your monthly income total is greater than your expenses, you'll soon be in trouble again. If possible, wait until you get yourself financially together and have enough income to support yourself. Then file bankruptcy, get rid of your debts, and have a bright future.

Of course, if your monthly income is greater than your monthly expenses, now may be the right time for you to file.

You have read the information in the three questions above to consider if you really wish to file bankruptcy. Now, here is one more consideration, and this is the "Big One." So hold on.

4. Exactly How Much Will I Wipe Out In Bankruptcy?

Bankruptcy may not wipe out all your debts. Some may be "non-dischargeable." On others, you will have to give up the item that the creditor holds as security if you want to cancel the debt. And then there are those loans from friends and relatives, which you'd like to still keep paying. So read through this section with us and see exactly how much of your debt you'll be actually wiping out.

a. Add up all your monthly debts;

b. Subtract all those debts which are non-dischargeable (see Section D, above);

c. This amount is your working total;

d. Though you can wipe out your entire working total, you may not want to.

EXAMPLE 1: If you have any secured debts and you want to keep the property the debt is secured on, you will have to continue making payments. For example, if you have a stereo set worth $1,000 and you only owe $200 on it, it would probably be worth keeping. (Read Section E, above, about secured property.)

EXAMPLE 2: If you owe money to a friend or relative, you may want to continue paying her.

So consider which debts you really want to get rid of, and which you will still be paying off after bankruptcy. Subtract the debts you expect to still be paying after bankruptcy from your working total.

e. The total you arrive at should be at least one-third of your monthly take-home pay. If you are a person who makes a low income, you may want to use the figure of one-fourth of your monthly take home pay instead of one-third. If the total is less, it is probably worth figuring out another way to deal with the bill collector. Keep bankruptcy in reserve until you hit the big time.*

EXAMPLE 1: Robert Benjamin of Eureka, California, has just gotten a divorce from his wife Karen. In the settlement he agreed to pay all the debts they contracted during their marriage.

---

* Of course, there will always be exceptions and special cases to this general guideline. For example, if your wages are being attached and there is no other way to stop, and you are afraid of losing your job, you may want to file bankruptcy, even if your total amount of debt is less than 1/3 or 1/4 of your yearly income.

He is also required to pay her alimony and child support. He is unable to pay all of his debts, and several collection agencies are preparing to attach his wages. He has a take-home income of $30,000 per year.

These are his total debts:

Alimony (monthly payment for February)	$	350
Child support (monthly payment for February)	$	500
Hospital bills	$	5,000
House	$	70,000
MasterCard	$	1,500
Automobile	$	5,800
Visa	$	1,000
Bedroom Set	$	4,200
Aunt Mae	$	1,400
	TOTAL	
	$	89,750

1. His total debt is $89,750.

2. Alimony and child support are "non-dischargeable" debts and so are subtracted from his total debts:

$ 89,750
$ - 850

TOTAL $ 88,900

3. His working total is $88,900.

4. Now he decides which of his debts he will still be paying after bankruptcy. He wants to keep the house ($70,000) and the car ($5,800), both of which are secured debts and both of which have a sale value in excess of the amount owed. He also wants to repay Aunt Mae ($1,400). These three debts total $77,200. Subtracting these debts from his working total:

$ 88,900
$ - 77,200

he gets

$ 11,700

5. If Robert files bankruptcy, he will actually wipe out $11,700. Since Robert is in bad financial shape and bankruptcy would free him of debts total more than one-third of his annual take home pay, he should consider it. By declaring bankruptcy he would wipe out his less important debts, and concentrate on paying spousal and child support, mortgage and car payments, and getting resettled.

Robert should consider one more thing. Under community property law, his former wife Karen is probably responsible to pay these debts if Robert does not, even though the divorce court awarded the debts to him and even if she never signed any agreement as part of the debt. If he files bankruptcy, she may get stuck (see Section G, above) and attempt to get him to reimburse her under the divorce decree. Robert should speak to a lawyer about this and see whether Karen should file with him.

▽ ▽ ▽

EXAMPLE 2: Anita Parker of Redlands, California, has an income (take-home pay) of $24,000 per year.

These are her total debts:

Dentist bills	$	275
Shortage oil credit card	$	150
Big John's department store	$	1,225
Back taxes	$	2,200
Traffic tickets	$	60
Piano	$	2,300
Friend Kathy	$	1,100
Old Datsun	$	1,400
Bank credit card	$	1,350
	TOTAL	$ 10,060

1. Her total debts are $10,060.

2. Traffic tickets and back taxes are "non-dischargeable" and so are subtracted from her total debt:

$$\$\ 10,060$$
$$\$ - 2,260$$
_____

TOTAL $ 7,800

3. Her working total is $7,800.

4. Now she decides which of her debts she will still be paying after bankruptcy. She wants to keep the piano ($2,300) which is secured property. She also wants to repay her friend Kathy ($1,100). These two debts total $3,400. Subtracting this amount from her working total:

$$\$\ 7,800$$
$$\$\ 3,400$$
_____

she gets

$$\$\ 4,400$$

5. If Anita files bankruptcy, she will actually wipe out $4,400. Since this is far less than one-third of her yearly take-home pay, Anita would be better off waiting and not wasting her power to file bankruptcy on such a relatively small amount. She should read through this book and see if she can come up with other ways to deal with her bills.

J. Ready to File?

1. See a Lawyer

There are simple bankruptcies and more difficult ones. Generally, we feel that if you intend to file bankruptcy, you can safely do it yourself. However, you should realize that a mistake like forgetting to include certain debts, or not putting your assets in order before you file, could be very costly. For some people, the fee you pay an attorney is probably worth the psychological security of having an "expert" handle the bankruptcy. (See our chapter on attorneys to help you pick one.)

But if your bankruptcy is a relatively simple one, you should be able to do it yourself. For those people with simple bankruptcies, or for the growing number who feel strongly that they want to handle their own affairs, or who can't relate to lawyers, we suggest you get a copy of BANKRUPTCY: DO IT YOURSELF, by attorney Janice Kosel (available from Nolo Press; see back of this book). This book contains all the forms and instructions necessary to do your own bankruptcy. You may also wish to have an attorney review the filled-out forms for accuracy. She shouldn't charge you more than $50-$100 for this service.

2. How Does Bankruptcy Work?

We won't go into much detail on how the filing of bankruptcy actually works. BANKRUPTCY: DO IT YOURSELF does that. But generally, here's what happens.

You list your debts and claims against you, your assets, and other general information in a petition which is filed with the federal court.

There is a $60 filing fee for each person who files, though it can often be paid in installments.

A few weeks later, a brief hearing with the trustee (the person who supervises your bankruptcy) and the creditors

will be held to give them an opportunity
to question you about any irregularities
in your petition. You must attend this
hearing. It is fairly informal and
normally lasts less than 15 minutes. If
either side claims that a serious and
unresolvable problem exists, there may
be a second hearing in the presence of a
judge.

If you have any assets which are not
exempt (see Section F), they will be
turned over to the trustee and divided
among your creditors.

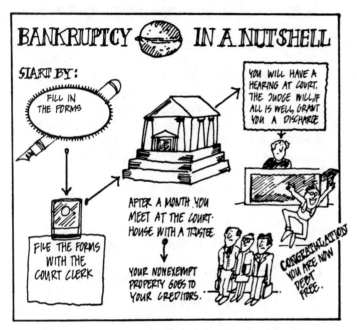

The trustee can also recover from
your creditors any extraordinary payments (normal monthly payments are okay)
you made or possessions you gave to any
of them within 90 days before you file
bankruptcy. If the extraordinary trans-
fer was to a relative, it can be ques-
tioned for up to a year. So during this
period only make those payments which
are essential (like your mortgage and
car payments). Don't pay off friends or
relatives, because they will probably
just have it taken away, which is more
painful than never getting it in the
first place. Also, don't give any of
your property away or sell it for less
than it's worth.

A few months later, you must attend a
court hearing. If all is in order, the
bankruptcy judge will inform you that
you have been given final discharge of
the dischargeable debts you had
listed.*

K. Reaffirming Your Debt

After you file bankruptcy, your creditors will soon be swooping down upon
you to get you to agree to pay off the
debt to them anyway--that is, to "reaffirm" the debt. They will use such
tactics as making you feel guilty, telling you that your credit rating is now
shot for life unless you agree to pay,
and persuading you that you need that
new vinyl sofa or piano or any other
secured property which they can take
back unless you agree to pay.

Be careful and make certain you don't
agree to anything without careful
thought. You are not required to keep
anything or even to talk to the creditor. Remember, you filed bankruptcy in
the first place to get rid of your
debts. If you do wish to keep some item
they can take away, bargain with them
for it. Never offer more than what it
is worth now, no matter how much you
owed them for it before bankruptcy.
For example, if you owed them $2,500 on
a secured piano and it is worth only
$1,500, offer them $1,500 or less if you
want to keep it. The creditor, even if
he says otherwise, is glad to get anything from you and will probably accept
your offer. But be careful. Don't let
them trick you into signing a new contract which says that if you fail to
make payments, they can reinstate the
full amount you owed before you filed
bankruptcy.

---

* In the unlikely event that you receive paper
from the court indicating that granting the bankruptcy would be a substantial abuse of the Bankruptcy Act, consult a lawyer immediately.

NOTE: If you do reaffirm a debt, it must now be approved by the court, and you may change your mind within 30 days.

At the hearing, the judge will consider whether reaffirming the debt is in your best interest--that is, the creditor didn't pressure you into doing it. The judge will also advise you of the effects of reaffirming the debt.

L. What About Your Credit Rating?

If you are considering bankruptcy, your credit rating is probably not that good to begin with. Bankruptcy is not likely to hurt it much. However, since the bankruptcy law has changed and made it easier for people to file bankruptcy, there has been a substantial increase in the number of people who have declared. As a result, creditors are much less willing to lend to you if you have declared bankruptcy. Don't be entirely put off, especially if you have a job or some income and can explain the circumstances surrounding your decision to declare bankruptcy.

Some problems may arise if you intend to buy a house or wish to keep a good rating with your credit union. Before a lending institution will take a mortgage on your home, they will probably check to make sure you can keep up with the payments. Your credit union may also wish to discuss you financial situation carefully, if you intend to continue using its services. Banks may also give you some guff if you want a loan.

M. Employer Problems

It doesn't seem that likely, but if you think your employer might get uptight and fire you if you file bankruptcy, mention the possibility of your filing to him and see her or his reaction.

If you intend to take a job where you must be bonded, such as a guard or bank messenger, you may have trouble getting the bond. Contact the Human Resources Development Department under California in the white pages of the phone book. They may be able to help you.

N. Still Worried?

If you are still worried about what might happen to you if you file bankruptcy, relax. So many people file bankruptcy each year that creditors have become accustomed to it. After all, bankruptcy is as much a part of the system as credit.

O. Chapter 13—Paying Off Your Debts

There is a program set up under the federal bankruptcy law which helps certain debtors pay off all or most of their debts with creditors or collection agencies. It is called Chapter 13 of the Bankruptcy Act. The bankruptcy court takes a certain percentage of each paycheck and divides it among your creditors, following the terms of your repayment plan. (Consumer Credit Counselors informally try to do much the same thing for you at a much lower cost. See Chapter 3, Section C.) The program usually lasts three years, though it may run up to five.

1. How It Works

The purpose of a Chapter 13 plan is to pay off your present debts over a three-year period. If you successfully complete the plan, all of your debts--except taxes and family support obligations--will be eliminated, even if you haven't paid off your creditors in full.

Generally, you shouldn't consider the plan unless your total ordinary living expenses equals no more than 80-90% of your monthly take-home pay. The remaining 10-20% can then be used to pay off the debts. You also need to consider whether the 10-20% will be sufficient to pay off the debts (or most of them) over the three-year period.

EXAMPLE: Tom owes $4,500. His take home pay is $2150/month, while his monthly expenses are $2,100. Since he only has $50 left over each month ($2,150 less $2,100), a Chapter 13 wouldn't help him pay off his debts of $4,500 over a three-year period.

But if Tom tries to cut back on his expenses (for example, by eating out less and buying fewer clothes), he figures he can save an additional $85 each month. He then multiplies this $135 monthly savings ($50 + $85) by 36 months (3 years) and gets a total of $4,860. Since his debts are $4,500, a Chapter 13 plan would now work for him. He will be able to pay off the full amount within the three years.

If instead of the above example, Tom had debts of $6,500, he could still file a Chapter 13 plan, and the $1,650 remaining unpaid after he completes the three years ($6,400 less $4,860) would be forgiven. But since his payments would not result in a payoff of 100% of his debts, he might want to consider whether there is really an advantage in filing under a Chapter 13 plan instead of straight bankruptcy. In either case, his creditors will not be pleased that he did not pay his debts off fully, and

his credit rating will suffer. See, CHAPTER 13: THE FEDERAL PLAN TO REPAY YOUR DEBTS by Janice Kosel. This book contains the forms and instructions necessary for you to prepare and file a Chapter 13 plan.

2. What It Does

A Chapter 13 plan stops all service charges, late charges, fines, collection charges, additional court costs, most interest charges and most finance charges. You can also arrange to stop wage attachments.

By filing a Chapter 13 plan you can keep most of your property. However, on secured debts you must pay the creditor either whatever the property is worth or the amount you owe, whichever is less. If you don't pay either, you must return the property. There are specific rules on 1) "purchase money secured debts" where the creditor sells you the pledge property or loans you the money to buy it; 2) "nonpurchase money secured debts" where you pledge certain property for a loan and the loan is not related to the property you pledge--for example where you pledge your furniture as collateral for a debt consolidation loan; and 3) secured debts on your personal residence.

Your boss doesn't have to know about your plan. However, even if your employer does know, it is unlikely that he or she will care. In fact, your employer may actually be relieved if your wages have been garnished and the plan puts a stop to it.

All governmental agencies are forbidden to fire you or deny you a license because you filed a Chapter 13 plan. But just as with bankruptcy, there may be a problem with employees who need to be bonded. Check with your employer if you are concerned.

3. Lawyer's Fee

The lawyer's fee is somewhere between $300 and $500, though you may be able to find one who will charge less (see Chapter 3). However, under the plan, your lawyer is treated as any other unsecured creditor of yours, receiving part payment each month. You cannot pay him or her in advance, nor can you make direct payments to him or her later on.

4. Student Loans

As we mention in Chapter 15, student loans are not dischargeable in bankruptcy unless they became due at least five years ago or paying them would impose an "undue hardship" on you and your family. They can be included in a Chapter 13, however. But if you are attempting to use a Chapter 13 to pay off only a tiny portion of your debts (see Section N2 above), you may have problems with student loans and should talk to an attorney or the trustee in the bankruptcy court before you file. Why? Because the bankruptcy court is aware of this Chapter 13 "escape hatch" on student loans, and will sometimes not allow a plan which is designed to accomplish what straight bankruptcy cannot.

5. You Can Still File Bankruptcy

Though Chapter 13 is written into the bankruptcy law, it is not the same as regular bankruptcy. Therefore, you can usually terminate the Chapter 13 proceeding and file a regular bankruptcy (providing you haven't filed bankruptcy within the last six years). You might want to do this, for example, if suddenly you got hit with some additional medical expenses or an automobile accident judgment or something else you cannot pay off under your Chapter 13 plan. Of course, filing bankruptcy will normally mean paying a lawyer another $300-$1,000.

On the other side of the coin, if you have filed bankruptcy within the last six years, and thus cannot file a regular bankruptcy, you can still use the Chapter 13 remedy.

6. Business Debts

Businesses which wish to file under a program similar to Chapter 13 can do so under Chapter 11 of the Bankruptcy Act.

If you are interested in filing under Chapter 13 as an individual but also have some small business debts, you should be able to include them with your personal obligations. See an attorney.

chapter 19

$ $ $ $ $ $

Frequently Asked Questions

In the several years since this book was first published we have participated in hundreds of lectures, classes and talk shows on radio and T.V. Many thousands of people have asked us many thousands of questions. Not remarkably, many of the same questions are asked again and again. At times we have almost felt as if somewhere there existed a Bureau of Wrong Information whose sole purpose was to confuse people.

Here are some of the questions:

Q. Is it true that if a collection agency accepts a payment from me after they have gotten a judgment on a particular debt, they can no longer attach my wages or other property?

A. No. See Chapters 8-12. If you owe money, the creditor is entitled to try and get it from you. If you are behind in your payments, he can take a payment (and often does) and still sue you, or if he has already sued you, still attach your wages. This may be nasty, but it's not illegal. If you wish to exact a promise from a creditor that he won't do some particular thing in exchange for a payment, get it in writing.

Q. I am six months behind on paying for my car and they are trying to repossess it. Can I stop them by starting to make monthly payments.

A. Probably not. This is a variation of the first question. Almost all written contracts have an "acceleration clause." This means that if you miss a payment the whole amount of the debt comes due. Once this happens you can't reinstate the debt by making future payments. Even making all past due payments can only reinstate your contract once, unless the creditor agrees otherwise in writing.

Q. Can I file for bankruptcy if I'm working?

A. Yes. In fact, the best time to file is when your financial situation will improve as a result. Obviously, this is true when you are working, since you can keep wages you earn after you file. See Chapter 18.

Q. What is the statute of limitations on student loans?

A. Six years on loans granted by the federal government and turned over to them upon default (Four years on non-federal loans in California.) But computation of the time can vary considerably. It may depend on when the federal government paid off the bank on your loan. See Chapter 15.

Q. Am I entitled to a statement of reasons if the bank refuses to grant me a loan or offers me a loan at terms I don't like?

A. Yes, absolutely. See Chapter 4.

Q. What can I do if I buy something with a credit card and the item turns out to be defective?

A. In most instances, you can refuse to pay the credit card company if the seller refuses to repair or replace it. See Chapter 14.

Q. Can I file Claims of Exemption against tax collectors?

A. You can on state tax claims but not on federal claims. See Chapter 16.

Q. Should I check my credit bureau file even if I am not interested in getting credit right now?

A. Since credit bureaus are notorious in having misleading or even downright inaccurate information, it is good if you check it out now, before it is given out to creditors or others. See Chapter 4.

□ □

APPENDIX

ATTORNEY OR PARTY WITHOUT ATTORNEY *(Name and Address)*:	TELEPHONE NO.:	LEVYING OFFICER *(Name and Address)*:

ATTORNEY FOR *(Name)*:

NAME OF COURT, JUDICIAL DISTRICT OR BRANCH COURT, IF ANY:

PLAINTIFF:

DEFENDANT:

CLAIM OF EXEMPTION (Wage Garnishment)	LEVYING OFFICER FILE NO.:	COURT CASE NO.:

—READ THE EMPLOYEE INSTRUCTIONS BEFORE COMPLETING THIS FORM—

Copy all the information required above (except the top left space) from the Earnings Withholding Order. The top left space is for your name or your attorney's name and address. The original and one copy of this form with the Financial Statement attached must be filed with the levying officer. DO NOT FILE WITH THE COURT.

1. I need the following earnings to support myself or my family *(check a or b)*:
   a. ☐ All earnings.
   b. ☐ $ each pay period.

2. Please send all papers to
   ☐ me.
   ☐ my attorney
   at the address ☐ shown above ☐ following *(specify)*:

3. I am willing for the following amount to be withheld from my earnings **each pay period** during the withholding period. **I understand that the judgment creditor can accept this offer by not opposing the Claim of Exemption, which will result in the following sum being withheld each pay period** *(check a or b)*:
   a. ☐ None
   b. ☐ Withhold $ each pay period.

4. I am paid
   ☐ daily ☐ every two weeks ☐ monthly
   ☐ weekly ☐ twice a month ☐ other *(specify)*:

NOTE: *You must attach a properly completed Financial Statement form to this Claim of Exemption.*
The Financial Statement form is available without charge from the levying officer.

I declare under penalty of perjury under the laws of the State of California that the foregoing is true and correct.

Date:

▶

_____
(TYPE OR PRINT NAME)

_____
(SIGNATURE OF DECLARANT)

Form Adopted by the
Judicial Council of California
982.5(5) [Rev. July 1, 1983]

CLAIM OF EXEMPTION
(Wage Garnishment)

CCP 706.124

SHORT TITLE:	LEVYING OFFICER FILE NO.:	COURT CASE NO.:

FINANCIAL STATEMENT
(Wage Garnishment — Enforcement of Judgment)

NOTE: *If you are married, this form must be signed by your spouse unless you and your spouse are living separate and apart. If this form is not signed by your spouse, check the applicable box on the reverse in item 9.*

1. The following persons other than myself depend, in whole or in part, on me or my spouse for support:

NAME	AGE	RELATIONSHIP TO ME	MONTHLY TAKE-HOME INCOME & SOURCE
a.		Spouse	
b.			
c.			
d.			
e.			

2. **My monthly income**
   a. My gross monthly pay is: . . . . 2a. $ _____
   b. My payroll deductions are *(specify purpose and amount)*:
      (1) Federal and state withholding, FICA, and SDI . . . . $ _____
      (2) _____ $ _____
      (3) _____ $ _____
      (4) _____ $ _____
      My TOTAL payroll deduction amount is *(add (1) through (4))*: . . . . b. $ _____
   c. My monthly take-home pay is *(a minus b)*: . . . . c. $ _____
   d. Other money I get each month from *(specify source)*:
      _____ is: . . . . d. $ _____

   e. **TOTAL MONTHLY INCOME** *(c plus d)*: . . . . e. $ _____

3. **I, my spouse, and my other dependents own the following property:**
   a. Cash . . . . 3a. $ _____
   b. Checking, savings, and credit union accounts *(list banks)*:
      (1) _____ $ _____
      (2) _____ $ _____
      (3) _____ $ _____ b. $ _____
   c. Cars, other vehicles, and boat equity *(list make, year of each)*:
      (1) _____ $ _____
      (2) _____ $ _____
      (3) _____ $ _____ c. $ _____
   d. Real estate equity . . . . d. $ _____
   e. Other personal property (jewelry, furniture, furs, stocks, bonds, etc.) *(list separately)*:

   e. $ _____

(Continued on reverse)

Form Adopted by the
Judicial Council of California
982.5(5.5), EJ-165 [New July 1, 1983]

FINANCIAL STATEMENT
(Wage Garnishment — Enforcement of Judgment)

CCP 703.530,
706.124

4. **The monthly expenses for me, my spouse, and my other dependants**

   a. Rent or house payment and maintenance . . . . 4a. $_____

   b. Food and household supplies . . . . b. $_____

   c. Utilities and telephone . . . . c. $_____

   d. Clothing . . . . d. $_____

   e. Medical and dental payments . . . . e. $_____

   f. Insurance (life, health, accident, etc.) . . . . f. $_____

   g. School, child care . . . . g. $_____

   h. Child, spousal support (prior marriage) . . . . h. $_____

   i. Transportation & auto expenses (insurance, gas, repair) *(list car payments in item 5)* . . i. $_____

   j. Installment payments *(insert total and itemize below in item 5)* . . . . j. $_____

   k. Laundry and cleaning . . . . k. $_____

   l. Entertainment . . . . l. $_____

   m. Other *(specify)*:

                                                                         m. $_____

   n. **TOTAL MONTHLY EXPENSES** *(add a through m)*: . . . . n. $_____

5. **I, my spouse, and my other dependents owe the following debts:**

CREDITOR'S NAME	FOR	MO. PAYMENTS	BALANCE OWED	OWED BY *(State person's name)*

6. Other facts which support this Claim of Exemption (i.e., unusual medical needs, school tuition, expenses for recent family emergencies, or other unusual expenses to help your creditor and the judge understand your budget) *(describe)*: *(If more space is needed, attach page labeled Attachment 6.)*

7. ☐ An earnings withholding order is now in effect with respect to my earnings or those of my spouse or dependents named in item 1 *(specify each person's name and monthly amount)*:

8. ☐ A wage assignment for support is now in effect with respect to my earnings or those of my spouse or dependents named in item 1 *(specify each person's name and monthly amount)*:

9. ☐ My spouse has signed below.
   ☐ I have no spouse.
   ☐ My spouse and I are living separate and apart.

I declare under penalty of perjury under the laws of the State of California that the foregoing is true and correct.

Date:

     . . . . ▶ _____
             (TYPE OR PRINT NAME)   *(SIGNATURE)*

     . . . . ▶ _____
       (TYPE OR PRINT NAME OF SPOUSE)   *(SIGNATURE OF SPOUSE)*

ATTORNEY OR PARTY WITHOUT ATTORNEY *(Name and Address)*:	TELEPHONE NO.:	LEVYING OFFICER *(Name and Address)*:
ATTORNEY FOR *(Name)*:		
NAME OF COURT, JUDICIAL DISTRICT OR BRANCH COURT, IF ANY:		
PLAINTIFF: DEFENDANT:		

CLAIM OF EXEMPTION (Enforcement of Judgment)	LEVYING OFFICER FILE NO.:	COURT CASE NO.:

Copy all the information required above (except the top left space) from the Notice of Levy. The top left space is for your name or your attorney's name and address. The original and one copy of this form must be filed with the levying officer. **DO NOT FILE WITH THE COURT.**

1. My name is *(specify)*:

2. Papers should be sent to

    ☐ me.

    ☐ my attorney (I have filed with the court and served on the judgment creditor a request that papers be sent to my attorney and my attorney has consented in writing on the request to receive these papers.)

    at the address ☐ shown above ☐ following *(specify)*:

3. ☐ I am not the judgment debtor named in the notice of levy. The name and last known address of the judgment debtor is *(specify)*:

4. The property I claim to be exempt is *(describe)*:

5. The property is claimed to be exempt under the following code and section *(specify)*:

6. The facts which support this claim are *(describe)*:

7. ☐ The claim is made pursuant to a provision exempting property to the extent necessary for the support of the judgment debtor and the spouse and dependents of the judgment debtor. **A Financial Statement form is attached to this claim.**

8. ☐ The property claimed to be exempt is

    a. ☐ a motor vehicle, the proceeds of an execution sale of a motor vehicle, or the proceeds of insurance or other indemnification for the loss, damage, or destruction of a motor vehicle.

    b. ☐ tools, implements, materials, uniforms, furnishings, books, equipment, a commercial motor vehicle, a vessel, or other personal property used in the trade, business or profession of the judgment debtor or spouse.

    c. all other property of the same type owned by the judgment debtor, either alone or in combination with others, is *(describe)*:

9. ☐ The property claimed to be exempt consists of the loan value of unmatured life insurance policies (including endowment and annuity policies) or benefits from matured life insurance policies (including endowment and annuity policies). All other property of the same type owned by the judgment debtor or the spouse of the judgment debtor, either alone or in combination with others, is *(describe)*:

I declare under penalty of perjury under the laws of the State of California that the foregoing is true and correct.

Date:

▶

· ·
(TYPE OR PRINT NAME)   *(SIGNATURE OF CLAIMANT)*

Form Approved by the
Judicial Council of California
EJ-160 [New July 1, 1983]

CLAIM OF EXEMPTION
(Enforcement of Judgment)

CCP 703.520

ATTORNEY OR PARTY WITHOUT ATTORNEY (NAME AND ADDRESS):	TELEPHONE:	FOR COURT USE ONLY

ATTORNEY FOR (NAME):

Insert name of court, judicial district or branch court, if any, and post office and street address:

PLAINTIFF:

DEFENDANT:

ANSWER—Contract ☐ TO COMPLAINT OF *(name):* ☐ TO CROSS-COMPLAINT OF *(name):*	CASE NUMBER:

1. This pleading, including attachments and exhibits, consists of the following number of pages: _____
2. DEFENDANT *(name):*

   answers the complaint or cross-complaint as follows:
3. *Check ONLY ONE of the next two boxes:*
   a. ☐ Defendant generally denies each statement of the complaint or cross-complaint. *(Do not check this box if the verified complaint or cross-complaint demands more than $1,000.)*
   b. ☐ Defendant admits that all of the statements of the complaint or cross-complaint are true EXCEPT:
      (1) Defendant claims the following statements are false *(use paragraph numbers or explain):*

      ☐ Continued on Attachment 3.b.(1).
      (2) Defendant has no information or belief that the following statements are true, so defendant denies them *(use paragraph numbers or explain):*

      ☐ Continued on Attachment 3.b.(2).
                                (Continued)

If this form is used to answer a cross-complaint, plaintiff means cross-complainant and defendant means cross-defendant.

Form Approved by the
Judicial Council of California
Effective January 1, 1982
Rule 982.1(35)

ANSWER—Contract

CCP 425.12

	CASE NUMBER:

4. ☐ **AFFIRMATIVE DEFENSES**
Defendant alleges the following additional reasons that plaintiff is not entitled to recover anything:

☐ Continued on Attachment 4.

5. ☐ Other:

6. **DEFENDANT PRAYS**
   a. that plaintiff take nothing.
   b. ☐ for costs of suit.
   c. ☐ other (specify):

_____   _____
(Type or print name)   (Signature of party or attorney)

How To Form Your Own California Corporation
All the forms, Bylaws, Articles, stock certificates and instructions necessary to file your small profit corporation in California.

California Edition $24.95
Texas Edition $21.95
New York Edition $19.95

The Non-Profit Corporation Handbook
Includes all the forms, Bylaws, Articles and instructions you need to form a non-profit corporation in California.

California Only $24.95

Bankruptcy: Do It Yourself
Step-by-step instructions and all the forms you need.

National Edition $14.95

Legal Care For Your Software
Protect your software through the use of trade secret, trademark, copyright, patents, contracts and agreements.

National Edition $24.95

The Dictionary of Intellectual Property Law
Provides functional and contextual definitions for the hundreds of law-related terms commonly used in high technology computer commerce.

National Edition $17.95

The Partnership Book
A basic primer for people who are starting a small business together. Sample agreements, buy-out clauses, limited partnerships.

National Edition $17.95

Plan Your Estate: Wills, Probate Avoidance, Trusts and Taxes
Making a will, alternatives to probate, living trusts, limiting inheritance and estate taxes, and more.

California Edition $15.95
Texas Edition $14.95

WillWriter - a software/book package
Use your computer to prepare and update your own valid will. Runs on Apple II+, IIe, IIc, the Mac, the IBM PC (and most PC compatibles).

National Edition $39.95

The Power of Attorney Book
Covers the process which allows you to arrange for someone else to protect your rights and property should you become incapable of doing so.

National Edition $14.95

Chapter 13: The Federal Plan to Repay Your Debts
The alternative to straight bankruptcy. This book helps you develop a plan to pay your debts over a three year period. All forms and worksheets included.

National Edition $12.95

Billpayers' Rights
Bankruptcy, student loans, bill collectors and collection agencies, credit cards, car repossessions, child support, etc.

California only $12.95

The California Professional Corporation Handbook
All the forms and instructions to form a professional corporation.

California only $24.95

Small Time Operator
How to start and operate your own small business, keep books and pay taxes.

National Edition $9.95

How to Settle a Simple Estate
Forms and instructions necessary to wind up a California resident's estate after death.

California Edition $19.95

How to Do Your Own Divorce
All the forms for an uncontested dissolution. Instructions included.

California Edition $12.95
Texas Edition $12.95

California Marriage and Divorce Law
Community and separate property, debts, children, buying a house, etc. Sample pre-nuptial contracts, simple will, probate avoidance information.

California only $14.95

The Child Support and Custody Handbook
How to increase alimony or child support, decrease what you pay, change custody and visitation.

California only $14.95

The Living Together Kit
Legal guide for unmarried couples. Covers wills, living together contracts, children, medical emergencies, etc.

National Edition $14.95

Sourcebook For Older Americans
Most comprehensive resource tool on income, rights and benefits of Americans over 55. Social security, Medicare, pensions, etc.

National Edition $12.95

How to Adopt Your Stepchild
How to prepare all forms and appear in court.

California only $17.95

A Legal Guide for Lesbian/Gay Couples
Raising children, buying property, wills, job discrimination and more.

National Edition $17.95

Start Up Money: How to Finance Your New Small Business
How to write a business plan, obtain a loan package and find sources of finance.

National Edition $12.95

Patent It Yourself
Complete instructions on how to do a patent search and file a patent in the U.S.

National Edition $24.95

How to Copyright Software
Covers common mistakes and how to correct them, failure to register, problems with protection and the Computer Copyright Act.

National Edition $21.95

The People's Law Review
50-state catalog of self-help law materials, articles and interviews.

National Edition $8.95

Fight Your Ticket
Preparing for court, arguing your case, cross-examining witnesses, etc.

California only $12.95

Legal Research: How to Find and Understand the Law
Comprehensive guide to doing your own legal research.

National Edition $14.95

Tenants' Rights
Everything tenants need to know to protect themselves.

California Edition $14.95
Texas Edition $6.95

Everybody's Guide to Small Claims Court
Step-by-step guide to going to small claims court and collecting a judgment.

California Edition $10.95
National Edition $10.95

How to Change Your Name
All the forms and instructions you need.

California only $14.95

Homestead Your House
All the forms and instructions you need.

California only $8.95

Author Law

Publishing contracts, copyright, royalties, libel and invasion of privacy. Includes index and glossary.

National Edition $14.95

The Criminal Records Book

Takes you through all the procedures available to get your records sealed, destroyed or changed. Forms and instructions.

California only $12.95

The Landlord's Law Book: Rights and Responsibilities

Covers discrimination, insurance, tenants' privacy, leases, security deposits, rent control, liability and rent withholding.

California only $19.95

The Landlord's Law Book: Evictions

All the forms and instructions you need to evict a tenant.

California Edition $19.95

Make Your Own Contract

Tear-out contracts for lending money, selling personal property, leasing personal proeprty, storing valuables, etc.

National Edition $12.95

The Independent Paralegal's Handbook: How to Provide Legal Services Without Going to Jail

How to open legal typing office to provide paralegal services

National Edition $12.95

California Civil Code

(West Publishing) Statutes covering a wide variety of topics.

California only $16.50

California Code of Civil Procedure

(West Publishing) Statutes governing most judicial and administrative procedures.

California only $16.50

Landlording

Maintenance and repairs, getting good tenants, avoiding evictions, taxes, etc.

National Edition $17.95

Your Family Records: How to Preserve Personal, Financial and Legal History

Probate avoidance, organizing records and documents, genealogical research. For existing and future family generations.

National Edition $12.95

Media Law: A Legal Handbook for the Working Journalist

Censorship, libel and invasion of privacy. Newsroom searches, access to news sources, reporter's privilege and more.

National Edition $14.95

How to Become A United States Citizen

Explains the naturalization process from filing to the oath of allegiance. Text is in both English and Spanish.

National Edition $9.95

All About Escrow

Gives you a good understanding of what your escrow officer should be doing for you.

National Edition $10.95

Annulment: Your Chance to Remarry Within the Catholic Church

Explains procedures by which Roman Catholics can obtain annulments.

National Edition $5.95

The Buyer's Guide: Inspecting a Home or Income Property

A realistic and practical approach to inspecting residential and income property.

National Edition $15.95

Homebuyers: Lams to the Slaughter

Describes how sellers, agents, lenders & lawyers are out to fleece the buyer & how to protect yourself.

National Edition $12.95

29 Reasons Not to Go to Law School

A humorous and irreverent look at the dubious pleasures of going to law school. $6.95

Murder on the Air

An unconventional murder mystery set in Berkeley, California. $5.95

---

self-help law books

Order Form

Qty.	Title	Unit	Total

Prices subject to change

Tax: (CA only; San Mateo, LA, Santa Clara & Bart Counties, 6 1/2%, all others, 6%

subtotal _____

tax _____

postage & handling _____

Total _____

name_____

address_____

_____

____Visa ____Mastercard

#_____ exp._____

signature_____

phone ( )_____

Credit card information or a check may be sent to NOLO Press, 950 Parker St., Berkeley CA 94710 or call (415) 549-1976

or

Send a check only to NOLO Distributing, Box 544, Occidental CA 95465